Eyewitness
FLIGHT

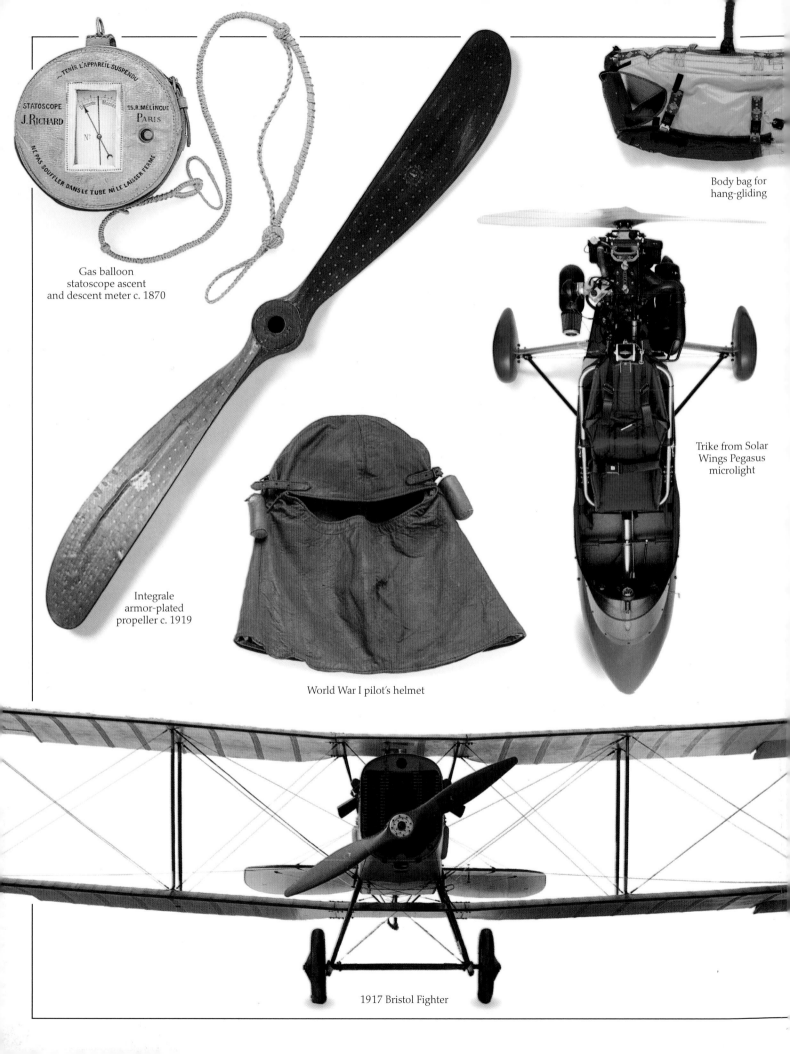

Gas balloon
statoscope ascent
and descent meter c. 1870

Integrale
armor-plated
propeller c. 1919

World War I pilot's helmet

Body bag for
hang-gliding

Trike from Solar
Wings Pegasus
microlight

1917 Bristol Fighter

Eyewitness
FLIGHT

Written by
ANDREW NAHUM

Spring pressure
airspeed indicator
c. 1910

1982 Schleicher K23
single seat glider

Black box
flight data recorder

Elliott pocket
altimeter c. 1910

1910 Anzani
fan engine

1927 Hawker Hart
pressed-steel
landing wheel

DK

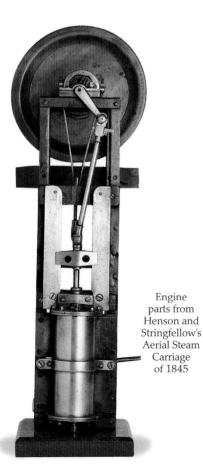

Undercarriage
from 1909
Deperdussin

Mach meter c. 1960

Engine
parts from
Henson and
Stringfellow's
Aerial Steam
Carriage
of 1845

Front fan from
Rolls-Royce Tay
turbofan engine

DK | Penguin
Random
House

1909 Paragon
experimental
propeller blade

Cockpit
from 1909
Deperdussin

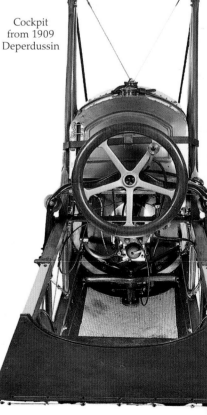

Project editor John Farndon
Art editor Mark Richards
Managing editor Sophie Mitchell
Senior art editor Julia Harris
Editorial director Sue Unstead
Art director Anne-Marie Bulat
Special photography Dave King,
Peter Chadwick, and Mike Dunning

THIS EDITION
Editors Sue Nicholson, Steve Setford, Jessamy Wood
Art editors Andrew Nash, Peter Radcliffe
Managing editors Julie Ferris, Jane Yorke
Managing art editors Owen Peyton Jones, Jane Thomas
Category publisher Linda Martin
Art director Simon Webb
Associate publisher Andrew MacIntyre
Production editors Jenny Jacoby, Andy Hilliard
Picture researchers Carolyn Clerkin,
Harriet Mills, Suzanne Williams
DTP designer Siu Yin Ho
Jacket editors Matilda Gollon, Adam Powley
US editor Margaret Parrish

This Eyewitness ® Guide has been conceived by
Dorling Kindersley Limited and Editions Gallimard

First published in the United States in 1990.
This revised edition published in the United States in 2011
by DK Publishing
1450 Broadway, Suite 801, New York, NY 10018

Copyright © 1990, 2003, 2011
Dorling Kindersley Limited
19 20 10 9 8
021—175428—Jul/2011

A catalog record for this book is
available from the Library of Congress.

ISBN 978-0-7566-7317-8 (Hardcover)
ISBN 978-0-7566-7318-5 (Library Binding)

Color reproduction by Colourscan, Singapore; MDP, UK

Printed and bound in China

A WORLD OF IDEAS:
SEE ALL THERE IS TO KNOW
www.dk.com

Contents

World War I
goggles

6
Flying like a bird
8
Lighter than air
10
Gliding aloft
12
Powered flight
14
The first airplanes
16
Those magnificent men
18
Double wings
22
The evolving plane
26
Light aircraft
28
Aero-engines
30
The propeller
32
Flying the world
34
Jetliner
36
Jet propulsion
38
Landing gear
40
Controlling the plane

42
In the cockpit
44
On the flight deck
46
Flying instruments
48
Rotating wings
50
Helicopter
54
Hot-air balloon
56
Airship
58
A modern glider
60
Kites for people
62
Portable planes
64
Did you know?
66
Who's who?
68
Find out more
70
Glossary
72
Index

Flying like a bird

Since the days of the mythical birdman Daedalus in ancient Greece, people have longed to take to the air. Some believed that if they could mimic the birds and their flapping wings, they too would be able to fly. From the Islamic inventor Abbas Ibn Firnas in about 840 CE and throughout the Middle Ages, many a reckless experimenter strapped on wings and lunged into the air from towers and clifftops—only to plummet to the ground, often fatally. Then, in the 15th century, the brilliant Italian artist and thinker Leonardo da Vinci applied his mind to unlocking the secrets of flight. Leonardo too believed that people could learn from the birds how to fly, but he realized that human arms are too weak to flap wings for long. So he sketched designs for flapping-wing machines called ornithopters. Centuries later, these sketches were discovered in his notebooks. As far as we know, Leonardo never tried to build his machines and, sadly, they would never have flown—imitating bird flight is far more complicated than even Leonardo understood. Nevertheless, his ideas may show one of the earliest scientific attempts to invent a flying machine.

FLYING DUCKS
In 1678, a French locksmith named Besnier tried to fly with wings that worked like the webbed feet of a duck. He was lucky to land alive.

THE FIRST FLYING ACCIDENT?
In ancient Greek legend, Daedalus was the craftsman who built the fabulous labyrinth for King Minos of Crete. Once it was built, the king threw Daedalus into prison to stop him from revealing its secret. Daedalus escaped with his son Icarus by soaring into the air on wax-and-feather wings he had made. In his excitement, Icarus flew so high that the Sun melted the wax and he plunged into the sea.

Sketches from Leonardo's notebooks

HOW A BIRD FLIES *below*
Most would-be aviators—including Leonardo—assumed that birds propel themselves through the air by flapping their wings down and backward, like rowing a boat. In fact, bird flight is much more complicated.

IN THE IMAGE OF A BIRD *left*
Leonardo's notebooks show how closely he studied birds to solve the riddle of flight—and how ingenious he was at devising mechanisms to flap the wings of his machines like a bird's. He thought birds used their wing tips to "squeeze" the air and propel them along. Leonardo did not fully understand how bird wings really work—indeed, we are still finding out today. It seems, though, that humans will probably never fly under their own strength by flapping.

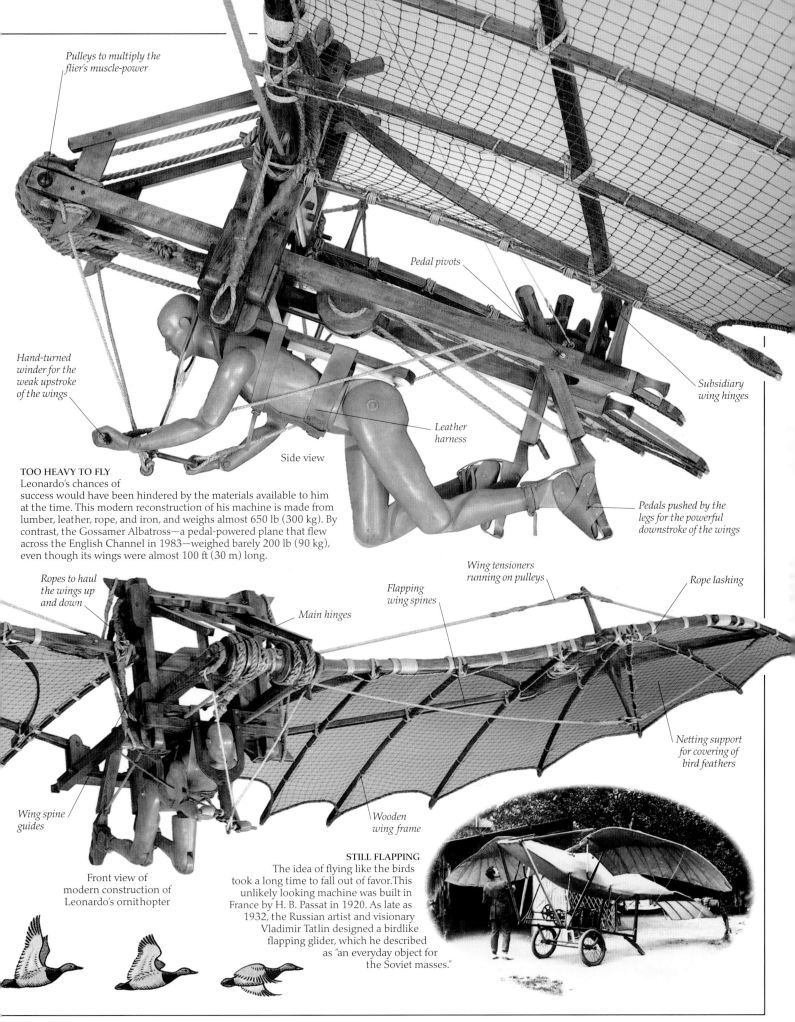

Pulleys to multiply the flier's muscle-power

Pedal pivots

Hand-turned winder for the weak upstroke of the wings

Subsidiary wing hinges

Leather harness

Side view

Pedals pushed by the legs for the powerful downstroke of the wings

TOO HEAVY TO FLY
Leonardo's chances of success would have been hindered by the materials available to him at the time. This modern reconstruction of his machine is made from lumber, leather, rope, and iron, and weighs almost 650 lb (300 kg). By contrast, the Gossamer Albatross—a pedal-powered plane that flew across the English Channel in 1983—weighed barely 200 lb (90 kg), even though its wings were almost 100 ft (30 m) long.

Ropes to haul the wings up and down

Flapping wing spines

Wing tensioners running on pulleys

Rope lashing

Main hinges

Netting support for covering of bird feathers

Wing spine guides

Wooden wing frame

Front view of modern construction of Leonardo's ornithopter

STILL FLAPPING
The idea of flying like the birds took a long time to fall out of favor. This unlikely looking machine was built in France by H. B. Passat in 1920. As late as 1932, the Russian artist and visionary Vladimir Tatlin designed a birdlike flapping glider, which he described as "an everyday object for the Soviet masses."

Lighter than air

THE FIRST FLIGHT
On November 21, 1783, Jean-François Pilâtre de Rozier and the Marquis d'Arlandes became the world's first aeronauts, when the Montgolfier brothers' magnificent blue-and-gold balloon carried them into the air above Paris.

Hoop or load ring suspended from a net looped over the gas envelope

IN THE END, it was not wings that carried people aloft for the first time. Scientists found that hydrogen gas, newly discovered in the 18th century, was lighter than air, and that hydrogen-filled soap bubbles floated freely. This suggested that a passenger-carrying hydrogen balloon might float in air like a ship on water. However, in 1783, the Montgolfier brothers, two French papermakers, made a huge paper balloon and filled it with hot air, which is lighter than cold air. In front of astonished Parisians, it rose majestically into the sky carrying two men. Ten days later, a second historic flight was made over Paris, this time by Jacques Charles and Nicolas-Louis Robert. Their rubberized-silk balloon contained hydrogen, which was to prove much more practical than hot air.

Short ropes suspending the basket from the load ring

FANTASTIC!
Over 400,000 people witnessed Charles and Robert's historic flight, commemorated on this fan.

BALLOON MANIA
Parisian society went "balloon mad" and snapped up mementoes of the new wonder of the age, such as this magic-lantern slide. Pulling the inner portion gave the illusion that the balloon was rising.

Strong rail to carry bags of sand ballast, which were jettisoned to reduce weight and maintain height

SOCIAL CLIMBING
In the late 19th century, ballooning became a fashionable society sport, and well-to-do gentlemen would compete for distance and height records.

SOFT LANDING
Early balloons often hit the ground with a sickening thud. Some carried wicker cushions strapped below the balloon basket to soften the blow.

GAS BALLOON
Gas ballooning was popular throughout the 19th century because flights could last for hours—unlike hot-air flights, which were over as soon as the air cooled. Gas balloonists had two control lines—one to let out gas through a valve at the top of the balloon for descending, and another to open the "ripping seam" to deflate the balloon once safely back on the ground.

Airships

The problem with balloons was that they simply floated where the wind took them. In 1852, Henri Giffard made a cigar-shaped balloon and powered it with a steam engine to make it dirigible, or steerable. Later, with gas engines and rigid-framed envelopes, such "airships" were the first large aircraft. By the 1920s, vast airships were carrying people across the Atlantic in ocean-liner style. But a series of disasters caused by the flammable hydrogen gas spelled the end for airships.

DIRIGIBLE MILESTONE
In October 1910, the French-built Clément-Bayard II became the first dirigible to cross the English Channel.

ZEPPELIN *below*
The German Zeppelin company led the world in airship-building. The World War I Zeppelins reached 660 feet (200 meters) in length and were about three times longer than modern jumbo jets.

World War I Zeppelin and a modern jumbo jet shown to scale

RIDING HIGH
Balloon races were immensely popular in the late 1800s. Professional aeronauts would often ride the load ring to make more room in the basket for joy-riding clients.

Pocket barometer c. 1909

UP AND DOWN *left*
In order to keep the balloon at a steady altitude, sand ballast had to be jettisoned to make up for the gradual seeping of gas from the envelope. But the balance was delicate. Throwing out too much ballast made the balloon climb, forcing the aeronaut to let out more gas—not only to bring the balloon back down but also because the gas expands at higher altitude and has to be vented. Constant venting of gas and jettisoning of ballast cut flights short, so early balloonists carried sensitive barometric (pressure-controlled) devices called statoscopes to tell them whether their balloons were rising or falling.

STATOSCOPE
J. RICHARD
"TENIR L'APPAREIL SUSPENDU"
25. R. MÉLINGUE
PARIS
NE PAS SOUFFLER DANS LE TUBE NI LE LAISSER FERMÉ

Statoscope c. 1870

Statoscope c. 1900

Anchor to tether the balloon during inflation

MAKING GAS
The hydrogen gas to fill balloons was made by dripping sulfuric acid on iron turnings in contraptions like this.

Basket made of wicker for lightness and resistence to landing shocks

PERCENTAGE OF HYDROGEN
CAMBRIDGE HYDROGEN INDICATOR
CAMBRIDGE INSTRUMENT CO.

GAS DETECTOR
Hydrogen is so flammable that it was vital to know if there were any leaks. This meter detected its presence.

Gliding aloft

FOR A WHILE, it seemed that the future of flight lay with balloons and lighter-than-air craft. But the British engineer George Cayley, at least, thought otherwise. He was convinced that wings, too, would one day carry people into the air, drawing his inspiration from a familiar plaything, the kite. Ingenious experiments with kites taught Cayley so much about how wings are lifted on the air that he was able to build a person-size version—the world's first real glider. Soon, other would-be aviators were trying their luck with gliders. It was all rather hit-and-miss, though, for no one had any real idea how to control their craft in the air. Then, in the 1890s, a brave young German named Otto Lilienthal built a series of small, fragile gliders—a bit like modern hang-gliders—and succeeded in making regular, controlled flights in them. His example proved crucial, and he has rightly been called the "world's first true aviator."

Tailplane

THE OLDEST AIRCRAFT?
Kites were probably flown in China more than 3,000 years ago, and arrived in Europe from there in the 14th century.

HANGING IN THE AIR
Photographs of Lilienthal gliding were published around the world, inspiring many imitators. His approach to flying was very scientific—he studied each problem with an analytical eye and tested each solution critically. Aviators should learn to glide, he insisted, and get "on intimate terms with the air" before taking the risky step of adding a motor—advice that was crucial to the success of the Wright brothers (p. 14).

George Cayley

GLIDING PIONEER
The invention of the airplane owes a great deal to the pioneering work of the English baronet George Cayley (1773–1857). It was Cayley who first figured out how a wing works, and all modern aircraft are based on the kitelike model glider he built in 1804, with its up-angled front wing and stabilizing tail. In 1853, at the age of 80, he built a full-size glider that is said to have carried his terrified coachman on a flight across a small valley.

PLANE IDEAS *below*
George Cayley (above) had ideas for many different flying machines, including an airship and this person-carrying glider, which he called a "governable parachute."

Wing cover of unvarnished cotton

Replica of Lilienthal's No. 11 hang-glider of 1895

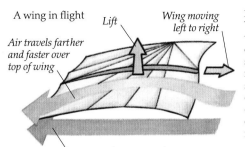

A wing in flight

Lift

Wing moving left to right

Air travels farther and faster over top of wing

Wooden spars to keep wing shape

Airflow (blue arrows)

HOW A WING WORKS

Wings are lifted by the air flowing above and beneath as they cut through the air. Air pushed over the top speeds up and is stretched out, so that the pressure here drops. But air flowing beneath slows down and the pressure rises. So, in effect, the wing is sucked from above and pushed from below. Even a flat board can give some lift, but pioneers like Lilienthal discovered that a cambered, or curved, surface is best. Today, wings are thicker and far more effective than those used by the pioneers. Research with computers and wind tunnels ensures that they are the right shape for each type of aircraft.

TRAGIC ACCIDENT
Sadly, Lilienthal was killed in 1896 while flying one of his gliders. The accident occurred not in town, as suggested by this engraving, but in open country near Berlin, when a gust of wind threw the glider out of control.

BRACED PAIR
The Wright brothers adopted the same braced construction as this biplane (two-winger) built by French-American Octave Chanute in the mid-1890s.

Willow hoop to act as shock absorber

Lilienthal supported himself on his forearms and controlled the glider by swinging his legs to shift its center of gravity

BELL'S KITE
Many pioneers believed that huge people-carrying kites had a future. This one was designed by the telephone pioneer Alexander Graham Bell.

Willow ribs

Powered flight

W$_{\text{ITH A GLIDER}}$, it was at last possible to fly on wings—but not for long. To fly any real distance, an engine was needed. By as early as 1845, two Englishmen, William Henson and John Stringfellow, had built a working model of a plane powered by a specially made lightweight steam engine—the only engine then available. No one knows whether their model ever really got off the ground, but it showed that the idea of a powered flying machine was no longer just a dream. Over the next 50 years, many imaginative engineers tried to get steam-powered flying machines airborne, both models and full-size airplanes. But steam engines proved either too weak or too heavy, and it needed the invention of compact, powerful gasoline engines for powered flight to become a real possibility.

EAGLE POWER
People had long known that a little more than human power was needed to fly...

"All-moving tailplane," or elevator

Silk-covered wings with 20 ft (6 m) span

Wing-brace

Rudder

Boiler

Engine pulley

Connecting rod

Steam tube

STEAM POWER
Henson and Stringfellow built a special lightweight steam engine for their model, with a boiler no longer than 10 in (25 cm). Heat for the engine came from a naphtha or spirit burner, and steam was raised in the row of conical tubes. (In the full-size version, the boiler would have had 50 of these tubes, but the engine was never built.) Steam from the boiler drove the piston up and down, turning the wooden pulley wheel. This, in turn, spun the two propellers via a cord drive belt.

Cylinder and piston

DID IT FLY?
Stringfellow built another model in 1848. To launch it, he ran it down a sloping wire for 30 ft (10 m) and then released it with the engine running. Some accounts say the model showed true powered flight by climbing a little before it hit a wall.

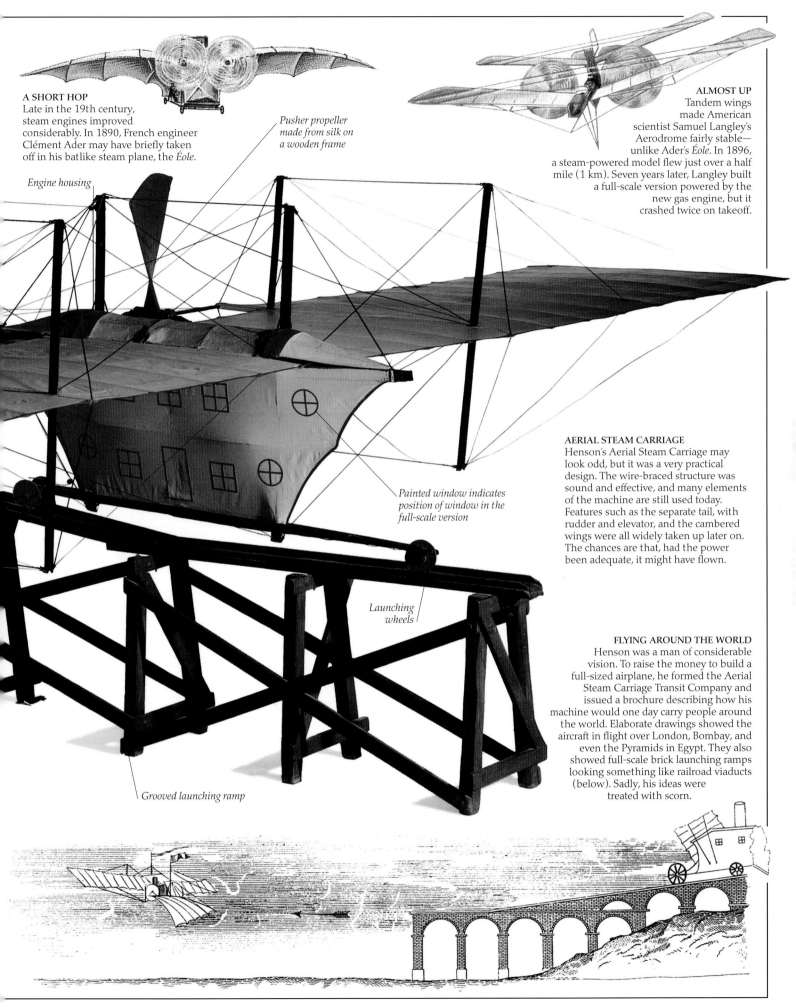

A SHORT HOP
Late in the 19th century, steam engines improved considerably. In 1890, French engineer Clément Ader may have briefly taken off in his batlike steam plane, the *Éole*.

Pusher propeller made from silk on a wooden frame

Engine housing

ALMOST UP
Tandem wings made American scientist Samuel Langley's Aerodrome fairly stable—unlike Ader's *Éole*. In 1896, a steam-powered model flew just over a half mile (1 km). Seven years later, Langley built a full-scale version powered by the new gas engine, but it crashed twice on takeoff.

Painted window indicates position of window in the full-scale version

AERIAL STEAM CARRIAGE
Henson's Aerial Steam Carriage may look odd, but it was a very practical design. The wire-braced structure was sound and effective, and many elements of the machine are still used today. Features such as the separate tail, with rudder and elevator, and the cambered wings were all widely taken up later on. The chances are that, had the power been adequate, it might have flown.

Launching wheels

FLYING AROUND THE WORLD
Henson was a man of considerable vision. To raise the money to build a full-sized airplane, he formed the Aerial Steam Carriage Transit Company and issued a brochure describing how his machine would one day carry people around the world. Elaborate drawings showed the aircraft in flight over London, Bombay, and even the Pyramids in Egypt. They also showed full-scale brick launching ramps looking something like railroad viaducts (below). Sadly, his ideas were treated with scorn.

Grooved launching ramp

The first airplanes

Wing made by stretching linen over a wooden frame and treating it to shrink it tight

ONE COLD THURSDAY in December 1903, at Kitty Hawk, North Carolina, the gas-engined flying machine built by the brothers Orville and Wilbur Wright rose unsteadily into the air, flew 120 ft (40 m), then dropped safely to the ground again. The world's first powered, sustained, and controlled airplane flight had been made. Reports of the Wrights' achievement met with disbelief in Europe at first, but their success was no accident. They had been methodically improving their designs—and, crucially, their flying skills—since 1899. When Wilbur brought the *Flyer* to France in 1908, it was clear that the Wrights were far ahead of the pioneers in Europe. But aviation was now progressing everywhere with astonishing speed. Sustained flights were soon almost routine. Then, in 1909, Frenchman Louis Blériot flew one of his elegant aircraft 26 miles (41 km) across the English Channel from France to England.

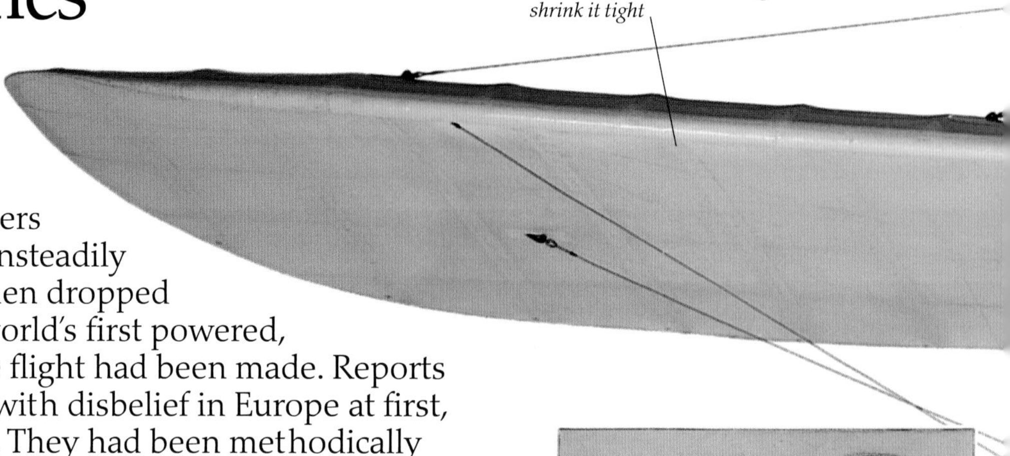

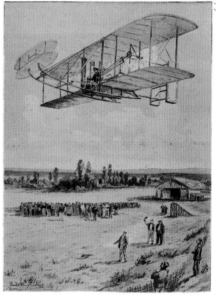

THE WRIGHTS' *FLYER* *above*
The Wrights realized that their plane needed some form of control to stop it from rolling from side to side. So the *Flyer* had wires to warp (twist) the wings to lift one side or the other. This meant it could not only fly level but also make balanced, banked turns, rather like a bicycle cornering.

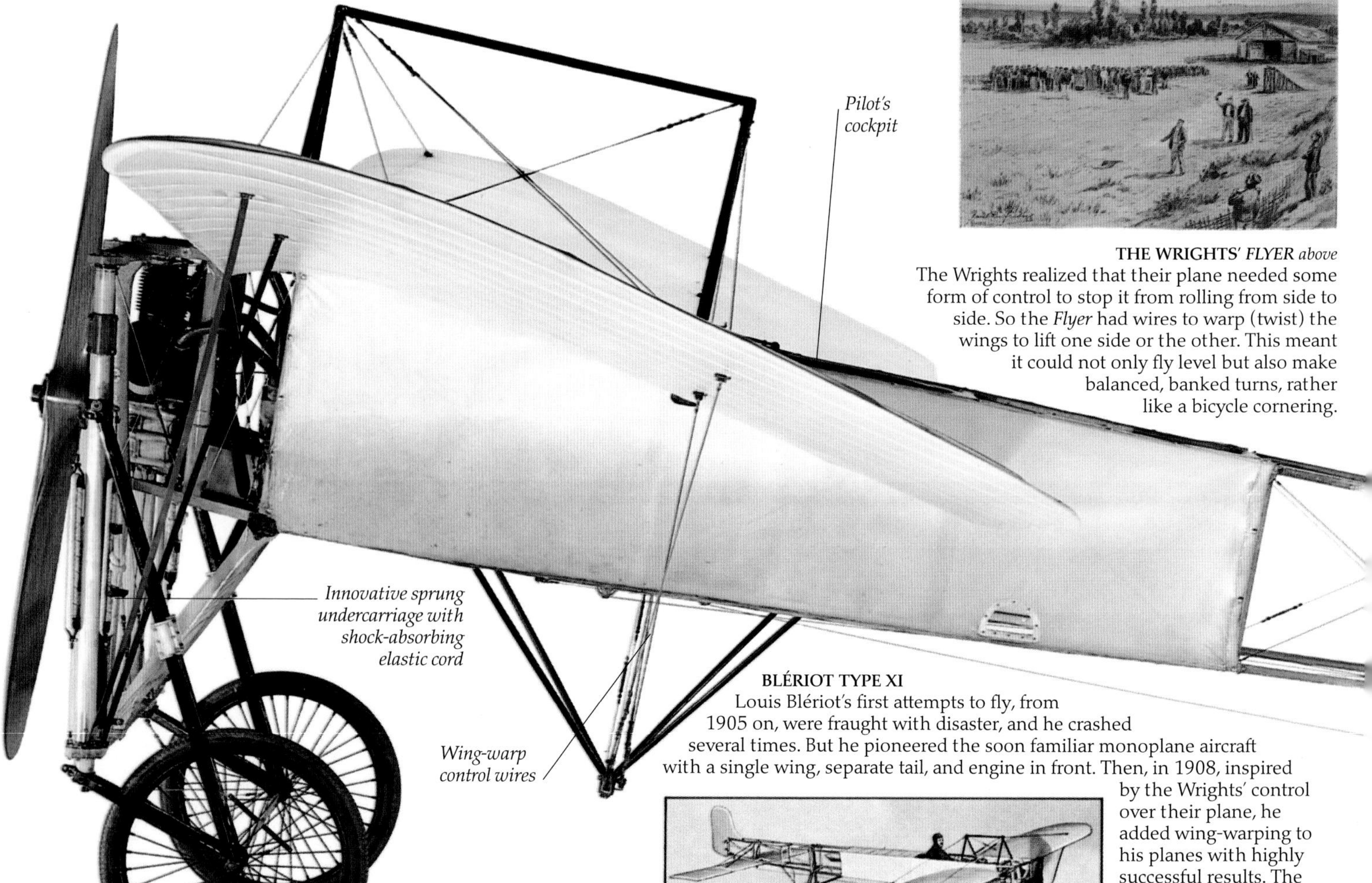

Pilot's cockpit

Innovative sprung undercarriage with shock-absorbing elastic cord

Wing-warp control wires

Side view of Blériot Type XI

BLÉRIOT TYPE XI
Louis Blériot's first attempts to fly, from 1905 on, were fraught with disaster, and he crashed several times. But he pioneered the soon familiar monoplane aircraft with a single wing, separate tail, and engine in front. Then, in 1908, inspired by the Wrights' control over their plane, he added wing-warping to his planes with highly successful results. The Blériot Type XI shown above is identical to the plane in which he flew over the English Channel on July 25, 1909 (left).

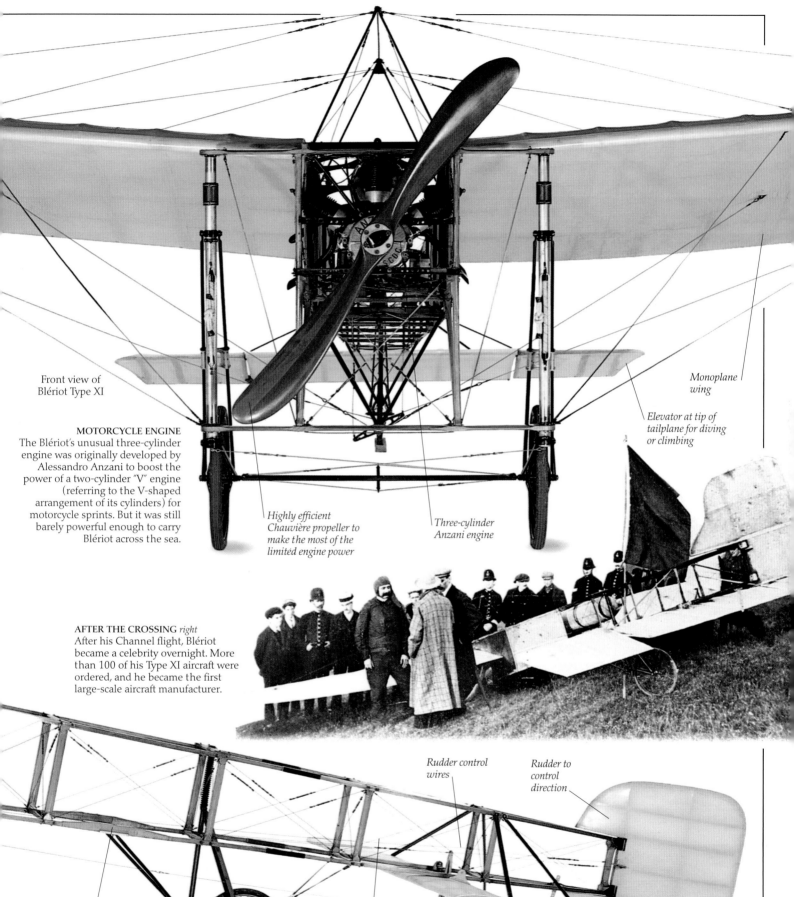

Front view of
Blériot Type XI

MOTORCYCLE ENGINE
The Blériot's unusual three-cylinder engine was originally developed by Alessandro Anzani to boost the power of a two-cylinder "V" engine (referring to the V-shaped arrangement of its cylinders) for motorcycle sprints. But it was still barely powerful enough to carry Blériot across the sea.

AFTER THE CROSSING *right*
After his Channel flight, Blériot became a celebrity overnight. More than 100 of his Type XI aircraft were ordered, and he became the first large-scale aircraft manufacturer.

*Highly efficient
Chauvière propeller to
make the most of the
limited engine power*

*Three-cylinder
Anzani engine*

*Monoplane
wing*

*Elevator at tip of
tailplane for diving
or climbing*

*Rudder control
wires*

*Rudder to
control
direction*

*Airframe made of
strong, flexible
woods such as ash,
hickory, and spruce*

*Bracing wires
in tension hold
frame together*

*Elevator
control wires*

Those magnificent men

THE FEATS OF THE WRIGHTS, Blériot, and various other brave and inventive pioneers created tremendous excitement, and aviation emerged as the sensation of the age. The daring young men who demonstrated their flying skill at air displays quickly became superstars. When a Parisian theater audience found in its midst Adolphe Pégoud— one of the first pilots to display aerobatics and loops—they stopped the show until he gave them a talk on aviation! Another pioneering French pilot, Louis Paulhan, was said to have earned over one million francs from his flying exploits. The early fliers deserved their fame, since their planes were difficult and dangerous to fly, and accidents were frequent. Sitting on an exposed seat was also uncomfortable and very cold, so warm clothing was essential. When Blériot crossed the Channel, he wore a coverall, but special flying gear was soon developed.

Soft leather

FINDING THE WAY
Pilots navigated by flying straight toward landmarks or following railroad tracks. A good set of maps was vital.

Warm wool lining

HOT FOOT
Warm boots were essential. These are soft, sheepskin-lined "fug" boots, originally thigh-length but cut down by the owner for convenience.

Thick rubber sole gave good grip when climbing aboard the aircraft

"WINDPROOF AIRMAN GEAR"
This suit from around 1911 could be lined with either fleece or quilt.

Flying gear c. 1916

World War I spurred the rapid development of flying gear. This selection was issued to pilots of the British Royal Flying Corps. Leather was thought the best material at the time, but it was soon replaced by one-piece Sidcot suits made of oilskin and lined with silk and fur.

*Fold-up collar to
keep neck warm*

Goggle-holders

HEAD IN THE CLOUDS
Cowl-type helmets with face masks
like this were sometimes used for
high-altitude flying. But some air aces
felt more alert flying without either
helmet or goggles.

GOGGLE-EYED
For most pilots, goggles gave vital
eye protection against the wind.
This pair is tinted to reduce glare
and made with shatter-proof glass.

*Leather gloves lined with
sheepskin mitten*

*Button-up
cuffs to keep
out wind*

HANDS
IN THE AIR
Stuck out in
the airstream
on the controls,
hands could
quickly suffer
frostbite if not
protected
by warm
gloves.

WINDPROOF
Higher speeds and
longer flights in World
War I meant suits had to
be more windproof,
particularly at the
neck, wrists, and ankles.

Double wings

THE EARLIEST PLANES had one, two, three, or even more sets of wings, and each arrangement had its supporters. But Blériot's cross- Channel flight in 1909 (pp. 14–15) showed just how effective a monoplane (single-winger) could be. Over the next few years, monoplanes tended to dominate in air races, because multiwinged planes suffered from extra air-resistance (drag). Unfortunately, these overstressed, competition monoplanes were too accident-prone and, in 1912, the French and British army authorities decided to ban monoplanes completely. They feared the single-wing design was weak, since, to give a similar lifting area to multiwings, single wings had to be very long. The best compromise between strength and low wind resistance seemed to be biplanes (two-wingers). So when World War I began in 1914, virtually all the fighters and observation planes were biplanes. The demands of war gave a tremendous boost to aircraft development. By the time the war was over, the airplane was a relatively sophisticated and reliable machine.

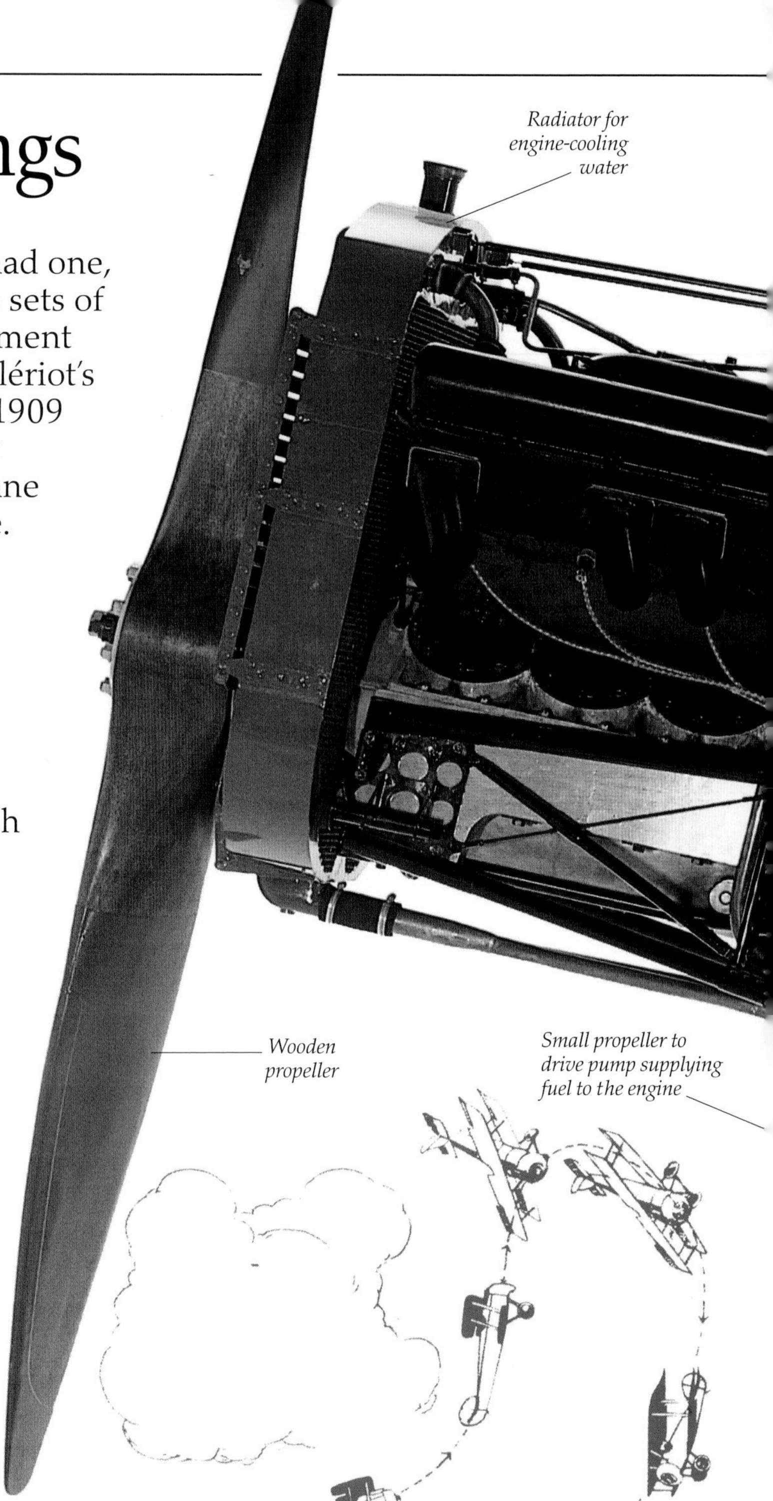

Radiator for engine-cooling water

Wooden propeller

Small propeller to drive pump supplying fuel to the engine

FOKKER TRIPLANE
Some triplanes (three-wingers) were built during the war. The German wartime Fokker Triplane was said to be "fearsome to look at and climbs like an elevator." It was also very maneuverable. But aerodynamic drag slowed triplanes down, and, by 1917, no airforce was using them.

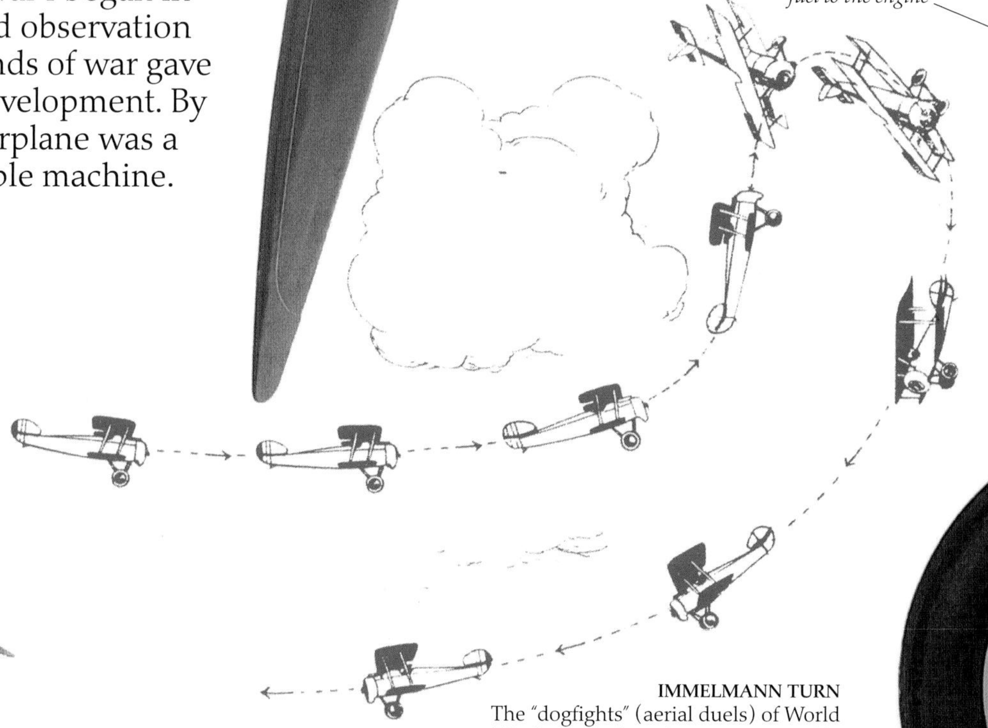

IMMELMANN TURN
The "dogfights" (aerial duels) of World War I revealed just how maneuverable planes had become in a short time. The Immelmann turn, named after the German flying ace Max Immelmann, was said to be a favorite way for pilots to evade pursuit or mount a hit-and-run attack. But it is unlikely that Immelmann or any other flying ace would have made themselves so vulnerable by flying upside down in front of the enemy's guns. It was probably just a simple steep climbing turn.

8-cylinder 300-hp Hispano-Suiza "V" engine

Vickers forward-firing machine gun aimed through a hole in the radiator

Timing device to ensure gun fires through the propeller only when the blades are horizontal

Control stick for climbing, diving, and banking

Pilot's seat

Rudder control wires

Rudder bar

Fuel tank

Ash frame

Bracing struts

Light wire landing wheels

Wing stubs

FIGHTING LIKE DOGS
Dogfights were fought between single-seat scout planes with forward-firing machine-guns. Since the pilot had to aim the whole aircraft at the enemy to shoot, flying skill was vital.

Bristol Fighter
c. 1917

In the early years of the war, the dangerous work of artillery spotting and observation was performed by slow two-seaters, often protected by faster single-seaters. When the British Bristol Fighter came on the scene in 1917, however, its powerful engine made it fast enough to act as both spotter and fighter.

Continued on next page

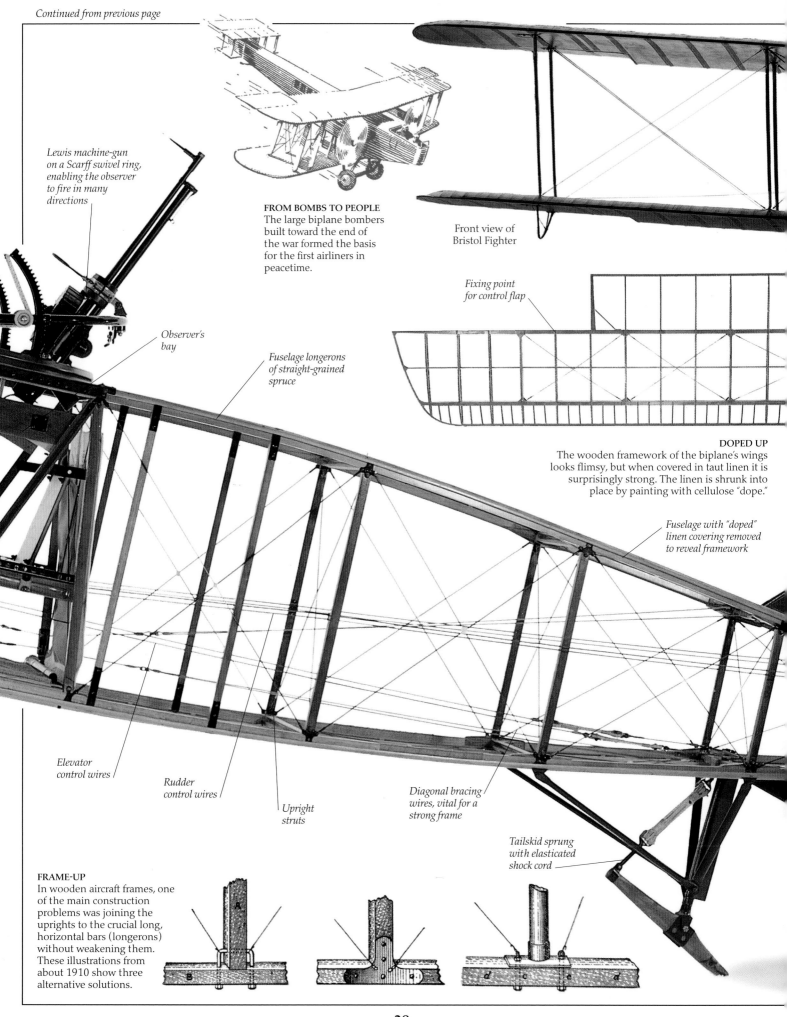

Continued from previous page

Lewis machine-gun on a Scarff swivel ring, enabling the observer to fire in many directions

FROM BOMBS TO PEOPLE
The large biplane bombers built toward the end of the war formed the basis for the first airliners in peacetime.

Front view of Bristol Fighter

Observer's bay

Fuselage longerons of straight-grained spruce

Fixing point for control flap

DOPED UP
The wooden framework of the biplane's wings looks flimsy, but when covered in taut linen it is surprisingly strong. The linen is shrunk into place by painting with cellulose "dope."

Fuselage with "doped" linen covering removed to reveal framework

Elevator control wires

Rudder control wires

Upright struts

Diagonal bracing wires, vital for a strong frame

Tailskid sprung with elasticated shock cord

FRAME-UP
In wooden aircraft frames, one of the main construction problems was joining the uprights to the crucial long, horizontal bars (longerons) without weakening them. These illustrations from about 1910 show three alternative solutions.

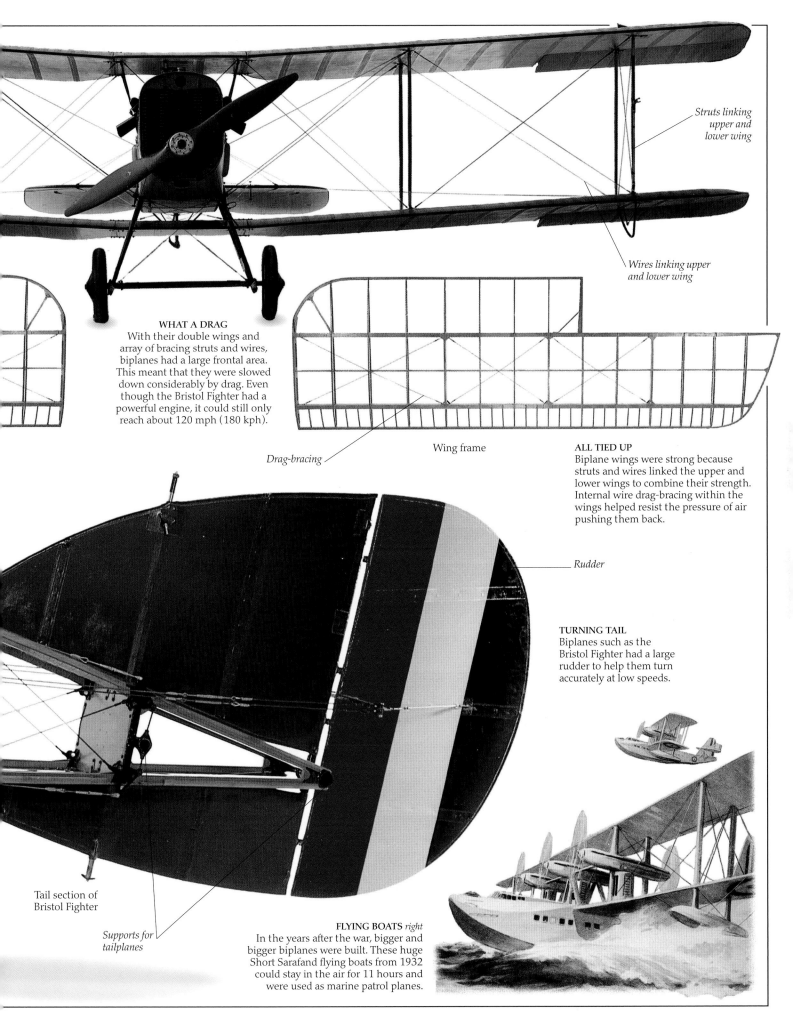

*Struts linking
upper and
lower wing*

*Wires linking upper
and lower wing*

WHAT A DRAG
With their double wings and
array of bracing struts and wires,
biplanes had a large frontal area.
This meant that they were slowed
down considerably by drag. Even
though the Bristol Fighter had a
powerful engine, it could still only
reach about 120 mph (180 kph).

Drag-bracing

Wing frame

ALL TIED UP
Biplane wings were strong because
struts and wires linked the upper and
lower wings to combine their strength.
Internal wire drag-bracing within the
wings helped resist the pressure of air
pushing them back.

Rudder

TURNING TAIL
Biplanes such as the
Bristol Fighter had a large
rudder to help them turn
accurately at low speeds.

Tail section of
Bristol Fighter

*Supports for
tailplanes*

FLYING BOATS *right*
In the years after the war, bigger and
bigger biplanes were built. These huge
Short Sarafand flying boats from 1932
could stay in the air for 11 hours and
were used as marine patrol planes.

21

The evolving plane

In the 20 years after the first international airshow was held in Reims, France, in August 1909, aviation progressed at an astonishing rate. The planes of 1909 were mostly frail, slow machines with flimsy, open wood frames, low-powered engines, and rudimentary controls. No plane at the airshow flew faster than 47 mph (75 kph) nor climbed higher than 500 ft (150 m) or so above the ground. Yet, within four years, aircraft were flying at over 120 mph (200 kph), climbing to 20,000 ft (6,000 m), and performing aerobatic feats such as loops and rolls (p. 41). By 1929, ungainly wooden planes were almost a thing of the past, and new all-metal planes with streamlined fuselages (bodies) and wings were hurtling across the sky at previously undreamed of speeds.

DEPERDUSSIN 1909
The French Deperdussin company was one of the most advanced aircraft manufacturers in the years before World War I, and its sleek monoplanes took many speed records. Despite this, the example above shows many features typical of the pioneering planes, with lateral control by wing-warping, (p. 14), a low-powered engine, and extensive wire bracing.

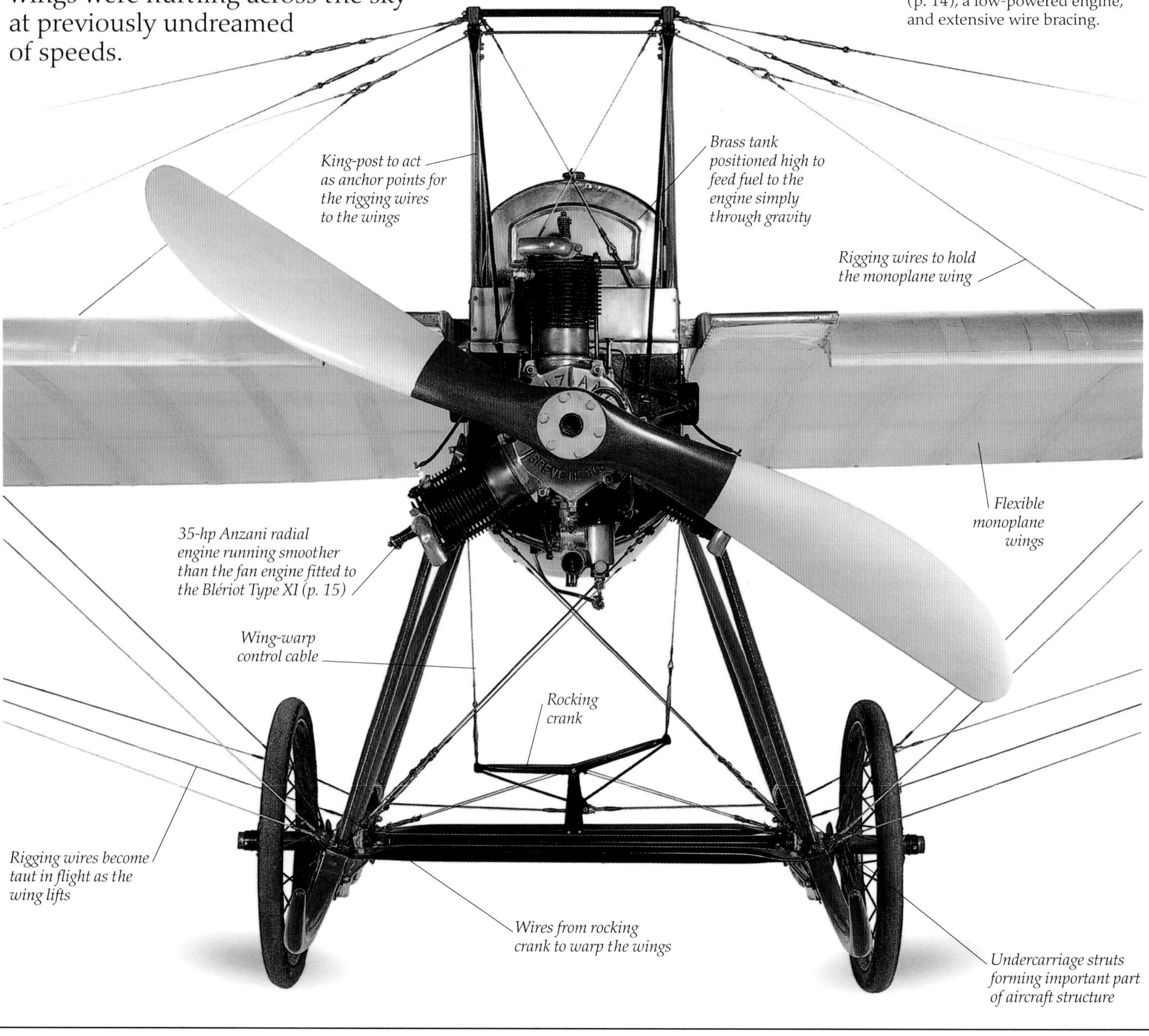

King-post to act as anchor points for the rigging wires to the wings

Brass tank positioned high to feed fuel to the engine simply through gravity

Rigging wires to hold the monoplane wing

35-hp Anzani radial engine running smoother than the fan engine fitted to the Blériot Type XI (p. 15)

Flexible monoplane wings

Wing-warp control cable

Rocking crank

Rigging wires become taut in flight as the wing lifts

Wires from rocking crank to warp the wings

Undercarriage struts forming important part of aircraft structure

SOPWITH PUP 1917

Aircraft improved immeasurably in the years before World War I, and wartime biplane fighters were faster and much more maneuverable than the flying machines of the pioneers. Lightweight rotary engines (pp. 28–29) propelled fighters such as this Sopwith Pup along at speeds of 115 mph (185 kph) or more, and improved control allowed planes to engage in dramatic dogfights. To bank the plane, the pilot no longer warped, or twisted, the wings but raised or lowered hinged flaps called ailerons on the tips of strong, rigid wings (p. 41). Fuselages were by now always enclosed. Toward the end of the war, a few manufacturers began to experiment with monocoque fuselages, in which all the strength came from a single shell rather than from internal struts and bracing.

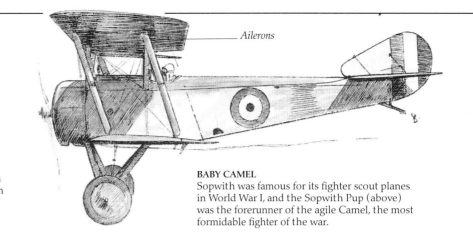

Ailerons

BABY CAMEL

Sopwith was famous for its fighter scout planes in World War I, and the Sopwith Pup (above) was the forerunner of the agile Camel, the most formidable fighter of the war.

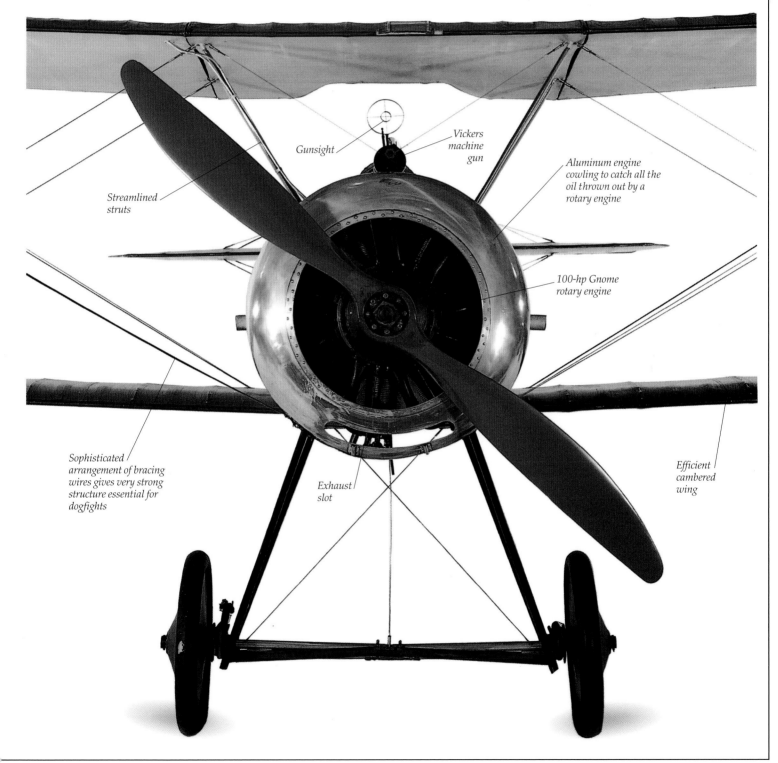

Gunsight

Vickers machine gun

Aluminum engine cowling to catch all the oil thrown out by a rotary engine

Streamlined struts

100-hp Gnome rotary engine

Sophisticated arrangement of bracing wires gives very strong structure essential for dogfights

Exhaust slot

Efficient cambered wing

Continued on next page

Continued from previous page

HAWKER HART 1927
Near the end of World War I, wood shortages persuaded many planemakers to experiment with metal, and they soon realized that metal was actually superior in many ways. Throughout the 1920s, air forces still preferred biplanes to monoplanes for their robustness, good handling, and low landing speeds. But fabric and wood wings were now frequently combined with metal monocoque fuselages. Very powerful engines and a more streamlined shape for both wings and fuselage meant that even biplanes could hurtle through the air at over 200 mph (320 kph) by the end of the decade.

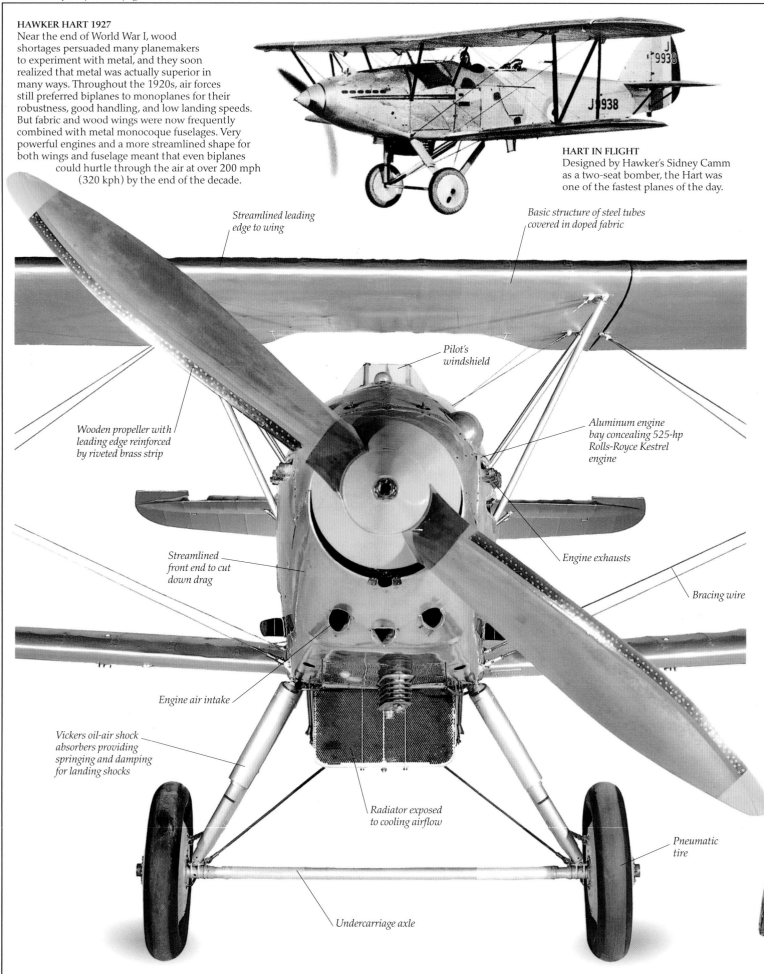

HART IN FLIGHT
Designed by Hawker's Sidney Camm as a two-seat bomber, the Hart was one of the fastest planes of the day.

Streamlined leading edge to wing

Basic structure of steel tubes covered in doped fabric

Pilot's windshield

Wooden propeller with leading edge reinforced by riveted brass strip

Aluminum engine bay concealing 525-hp Rolls-Royce Kestrel engine

Streamlined front end to cut down drag

Engine exhausts

Bracing wire

Engine air intake

Vickers oil-air shock absorbers providing springing and damping for landing shocks

Radiator exposed to cooling airflow

Pneumatic tire

Undercarriage axle

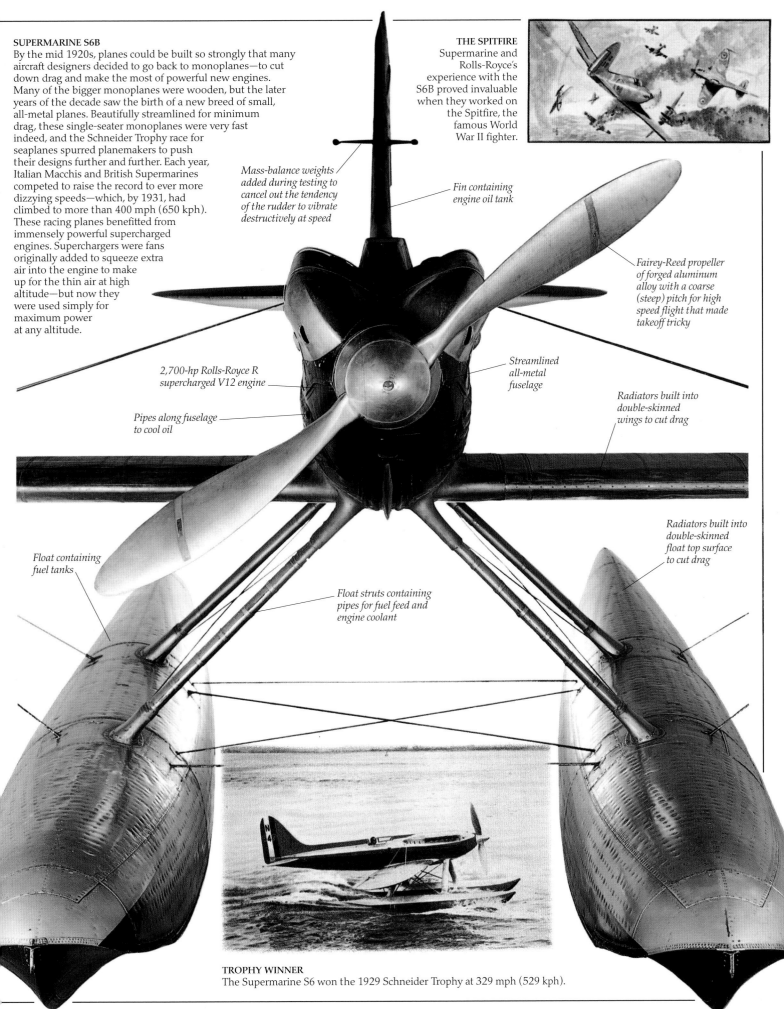

SUPERMARINE S6B

By the mid 1920s, planes could be built so strongly that many aircraft designers decided to go back to monoplanes—to cut down drag and make the most of powerful new engines. Many of the bigger monoplanes were wooden, but the later years of the decade saw the birth of a new breed of small, all-metal planes. Beautifully streamlined for minimum drag, these single-seater monoplanes were very fast indeed, and the Schneider Trophy race for seaplanes spurred planemakers to push their designs further and further. Each year, Italian Macchis and British Supermarines competed to raise the record to ever more dizzying speeds—which, by 1931, had climbed to more than 400 mph (650 kph). These racing planes benefitted from immensely powerful supercharged engines. Superchargers were fans originally added to squeeze extra air into the engine to make up for the thin air at high altitude—but now they were used simply for maximum power at any altitude.

THE SPITFIRE
Supermarine and Rolls-Royce's experience with the S6B proved invaluable when they worked on the Spitfire, the famous World War II fighter.

Mass-balance weights added during testing to cancel out the tendency of the rudder to vibrate destructively at speed

Fin containing engine oil tank

Fairey-Reed propeller of forged aluminum alloy with a coarse (steep) pitch for high speed flight that made takeoff tricky

2,700-hp Rolls-Royce R supercharged V12 engine

Streamlined all-metal fuselage

Pipes along fuselage to cool oil

Radiators built into double-skinned wings to cut drag

Radiators built into double-skinned float top surface to cut drag

Float containing fuel tanks

Float struts containing pipes for fuel feed and engine coolant

TROPHY WINNER
The Supermarine S6 won the 1929 Schneider Trophy at 329 mph (529 kph).

Light aircraft

SINGLE-ENGINED LIGHT PLANES are today flown all over the world for training pilots, for basic transportation in remote places, and for the sheer pleasure of flying. They are very simple aircraft with, typically, a fixed undercarriage, a monoplane wing above the cabin, simple fuselage and tail, and a small gas engine to turn the propeller at the front. Usually very conventional in design, they work in much the same way as the planes of the pioneers. Only the materials are genuinely new, with aluminum alloys and plastics replacing the traditional wood and linen.

EPIC FLIGHT
The most famous light plane was the *Spirit of St. Louis*, in which Charles Lindbergh flew solo across the Atlantic in 1927.

Fuel tank holding enough fuel for 2.5 hours or 120 miles (190 km) of flying

Tiny, two-cylinder Rotax engine

SNOWBIRD
The basic shape of light planes has changed little since World War II, and the main elements of planes like the Snowbird have long been familiar to pilots. The Snowbird incorporates developments in ultralights (pp. 62–63), resulting in a light plane costing little more than a family car.

GAS POWER
While bigger, faster planes now usually have jet engines, gas engines are quite adequate for light planes.

Cabin superstructure of light aluminum, with roof forming wing mounts

Fixed undercarriage

Propeller is made of laminated wood

ON THE PANEL *below*
On the Snowbird's instrument panel, digital electronic displays replace the clocks and cables traditionally used on light planes.

Wingfront is a D-shaped box, made of sheet alloy, that resists twisting

WEIGHTLIFTER
Wings are specially designed for each plane to give just the right amount of lift. The length of the wing (its span) and its cross-section (camber) are critical. Wings must also be light and very strong, too. The stresses placed on the wings of even the lightest, slowest plane as it flies through the air are considerable. The Snowbird's wing of fabric stretched over an aluminum frame is unusually simple. But the cross-struts and bracing pieces had to be very carefully designed.

AIR SCREW *above*
Most light planes have a traditional twin-bladed propeller. This is mounted at the front, to pull the aircraft forward.

Absence of ailerons makes wing frame very simple

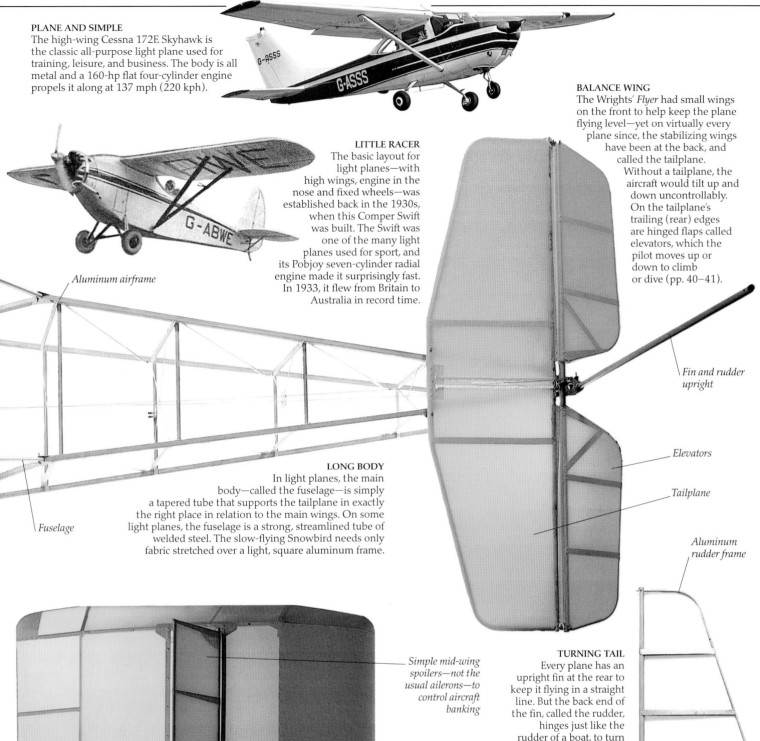

PLANE AND SIMPLE
The high-wing Cessna 172E Skyhawk is the classic all-purpose light plane used for training, leisure, and business. The body is all metal and a 160-hp flat four-cylinder engine propels it along at 137 mph (220 kph).

BALANCE WING
The Wrights' *Flyer* had small wings on the front to help keep the plane flying level—yet on virtually every plane since, the stabilizing wings have been at the back, and called the tailplane. Without a tailplane, the aircraft would tilt up and down uncontrollably. On the tailplane's trailing (rear) edges are hinged flaps called elevators, which the pilot moves up or down to climb or dive (pp. 40–41).

LITTLE RACER
The basic layout for light planes—with high wings, engine in the nose and fixed wheels—was established back in the 1930s, when this Comper Swift was built. The Swift was one of the many light planes used for sport, and its Pobjoy seven-cylinder radial engine made it surprisingly fast. In 1933, it flew from Britain to Australia in record time.

Aluminum airframe

Fin and rudder upright

LONG BODY
In light planes, the main body—called the fuselage—is simply a tapered tube that supports the tailplane in exactly the right place in relation to the main wings. On some light planes, the fuselage is a strong, streamlined tube of welded steel. The slow-flying Snowbird needs only fabric stretched over a light, square aluminum frame.

Elevators

Tailplane

Fuselage

Aluminum rudder frame

Simple mid-wing spoilers—not the usual ailerons—to control aircraft banking

Special plastic film, shrunk tightly over the aircraft frame with a heat gun

TURNING TAIL
Every plane has an upright fin at the rear to keep it flying in a straight line. But the back end of the fin, called the rudder, hinges just like the rudder of a boat, to turn the plane left or right. Steering a plane in the air, however, is not as simple as steering a boat, and the pilot has to use the ailerons, or spoilers, on the main wings as well (pp. 40–41).

COMPLETE PLANE
The finished Snowbird is so light and stable that it stalls, or stops flying, only when the speed drops as low as 34 mph (55 kph).

Aero-engines

VITAL SPARK
Like a car engine, aircraft piston engines have spark plugs to ignite the fuel charge to drive the piston down in each cylinder.

POWERED FLIGHT only became a real possibility with the development of piston engines for cars in the early years of the 20th century. Indeed, many pioneering machines were propelled into the air by engines taken straight from cars and motorcycles and modified by ingenious aviators. Unfortunately, air-cooled motorcycle engines often lost power or seized up in midflight, while water-cooled car engines were very heavy. Before long, aviators began to build their own engines, and they made them both light and extremely powerful. From then on, piston engines for aircraft became ever more powerful and sophisticated until, soon after World War II, the coming of jet engines meant that piston engines were used only on light planes (pp. 26–27).

Carburetor

Exhaust

Copper cooling jacket around the cylinder

COOL JACKET
To save weight, some big, water-cooled aero-engines, such as this ENV from around 1910, had very thin copper water jackets coated electrically onto the cylinders.

Cylinder cut away to reveal piston

Pipe to carry a mixture of fuel and air from the carburetor to the cylinders

Piston—driven down the cylinder by burning fuel and back up again by the rotating crankshaft

Crankcase containing crankshaft turned by the pistons

Flange for exhaust pipe

Cast-iron cylinders with fins to improve cooling by increasing the area of metal exposed to the airflow

WHEELS TO WINGS
Like many early aero-engines, this 1910 Anzani "fan" type engine (with the cylinders spread out in a fan shape) came from a motorcycle. Anzani had originally put the extra cylinder in the middle of their V-twin engine to gain power for motorcycle sprints and hill-climbs. This was the kind of engine used by Blériot for his Channel crossing in 1909 (pp. 14–15). Its output of 25 hp was barely adequate for the task, and the engine would have seized up, so it is said, if a timely shower of rain had not cooled it down.

Float to control the level of fuel in the carburetor

Carburetor to deliver fuel to the cylinders at the right rate

Propeller mounted here and turned by the crankshaft

ROTARY ENGINE
The cylinders on the earliest aero-engines were either arranged in-line and needed heavy water-cooling systems, or set in a circle (radially) and did not cool well at all. So, in 1909, the French Séguin brothers introduced the rotary engine. As in a radial, the rotary's cylinders were arranged in a ring; but, unlike the radial, the cylinders went around with the propeller, while the central crank stayed still.

Crankshaft, which alone stays still while the cylinders rotate around it

Inlet pipes channeling the fuel and air mixture from the crankcase to the cylinders

Valves to let fuel in and burned gases (exhaust) out

Cylinders kept especially cool by the flow of air around them as they rotate

Crankcase rotates with the cylinders

Finely machined cylinders with light, thin walls only 0.04 in (1 mm) thick

Connecting rods to pistons are all joined to a single bearing around the crankshaft

AERO-GIANT
Not all propeller planes were powered by piston engines. The huge Saunders-Roe Princess flying-boat had six big turboprop jet engines (p. 36) to turn 12 propellers.

LIGHT POWER
This WAE 342 Hurricane engine weighs only 18 lb (8.4 kg), yet it produces as much power as Blériot's 1908 Anzani, which weighed over 150 lb (70 kg). Originally designed for light planes, it is now used to power remote-controlled drones for gunnery and antiaircraft practice.

Carburetor

Propeller shaft

Cylinder

The propeller

PROPELLERS SEEM TO HAVE changed little since the pioneering days. Yet, as the Wright brothers were quick to appreciate, they are not simply oars for the air; they are like spinning wings that thrust the plane forward in much the same way as wings lift it upward. So the shape of a propeller is as crucial to performance as the shape of a wing, and the subtle evolution of propeller design over the years has improved efficiency dramatically. Propellers have gained in strength, too, as construction has changed from laminations (layers) of wood to forged aluminum, to cope with the steadily increasing power of aero-engines.

WRIGHT 1909
The Wright brothers built their own wind tunnel for testing wings and propellers. This design shows they knew that the blade had to be twisted to give it a shallower angle at the tip.

PHILLIPS 1893
This early propeller, designed by English aerofoil (wing-shape) expert Horatio Phillips, looks a little like a ship's screw. Yet it worked well, once lifting a tethered experimental aircraft weighing 400 lb (180 kg).

Propeller blade made from strips of mood

Blade angle (pitch) steeper closer to the hub

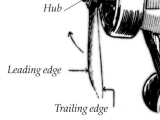

Tip travels farther and faster than hub

Propeller rotates this way

Hub

Leading edge

Trailing edge

PARAGON 1909
The profile of this experimental blade is good, but there was no need for such a sweeping shape at the slow spinning speeds of the time.

PITCH AND TWIST
The thrust developed by a propeller varies with its speed and the angle at which its blades carve through the air—its pitch. Because the propeller tip spins faster than the hub, the blade is twisted to make the pitch steep near the hub but shallower toward the tip. This keeps thrust even all the way along the blade.

Brass cover to protect the blade from sea spray

LANG 1917
Long and robust, this laminated propeller was made to cope with the power of a 225-hp Sunbeam engine on a Short 184 seaplane. The brass-clad tips protect it from erosion by sea spray.

WOTAN 1917
The laminated construction can be seen in this elegant German propeller. The propeller was made by glueing roughly shaped laminations together and then carving them to form a smoothly tapered aerofoil.

EXTRA BLADES
As engine power increased, propellers were made with three or four blades to cope with the extra load.

Rivets to hold the brass armor to the blade

Laminations of spruce and ash

Swivel to vary the pitch of the blades

HELE-SHAW-BEACHAM 1928
Ideally, an aircraft needs coarse (steeply) pitched propellers for cruising at speed and fine (shallow) pitch for good thrust at takeoff. In the late 1920s, many aircraft began using variable pitch propellers, on which the angle of the blades could be changed to suit the conditions. This particular propeller was operated by engine oil pressure.

FAIREY-REED 1922
As aircraft designers tried to get planes to go faster and faster in the years after World War I, they demanded thinner blades to slice easily through the air. Thin wooden blades were too weak to take the strain, but in 1920, Sylvanus Albert Reed developed a way of making strong propellers from forged aluminum. Over the years, these gradually replaced laminated wooden propellers.

INTEGRALE 1919
The brass sheath covering this wooden-bladed propeller was designed to protect it from enemy attack. Before the interruptor gear was invented (pp. 18–19), propellers on some French fighter planes had even heavier armor-plating to stop them from being destroyed by their own forward-firing machine-gun.

Swiveling blade to give the right pitch for both landing and high-speed cruising

UNDUCTED FAN
To save fuel and weight, some jet manufacturers have tried adding propellers, known as unducted fans, to their engines. So far, unducted fans have proved too noisy to be practical.

Flying the world

THE TIME BETWEEN the two world wars was the heroic age of aviation—the age of the first nonstop crossing of the Atlantic by Alcock and Brown (p. 42), Lindbergh's solo crossing (p. 26), and Australian aviator Charles Kingsford Smith's epic flight over the Pacific in 1928. Feats like these inspired confidence in aviation, and soon planes began to carry passengers regularly. All over the world, new airlines went into business, and more and more people experienced the speed and novelty of flying. Air travel grew most rapidly in the United States, where mail contracts helped finance the emerging airlines. Here, especially, passenger-aircraft design made rapid progress and, in 1933, Boeing launched the 247, the world's first modern airliner.

STARS IN THE SKY
Air travel was a glamorous new experience, and many of the first passengers on the prestigious London to Paris route were American movie stars or sports celebrities.

CROYDON AIRPORT
Early airports were often little more than a grass landing-strip and a straggle of tents. The world's first modern airport buildings were built at Croydon, near London, England, in 1928.

Flight deck with automatic pilot to reduce stress on the pilot during long flights—a very advanced feature for the 1930s

Metal skin of the plane made strong enough ("stressed") for bracing wires and struts to be unnecessary

THIS IS YOUR CAPTAIN
When Britain's Instone shipping line launched an airline in 1919, their pilots wore the blue uniforms of a ship's captain. This is now standard dress for airline pilots.

BOEING 247D
The Boeing 247D was one of the most advanced planes of its time. It had smooth monoplane wings, a streamlined, all-metal "skin," and an undercarriage that retracted into the wing during flight. All this helped cut aerodynamic drag so much that the 247D could fly at almost 180 mph (300 kph)—faster than most fighter planes of the time. Passengers could be whisked right across the United States in less than 20 hours.

Pressure tube for airspeed indicator

Front view of Boeing 247D

Boeing 247D in flight with undercarriage retracted

N18E

De Havilland Dragon

HARDY TRAVELERS
Early passenger planes were tiny in comparison to those of today. The de Havilland Dragon of 1933 (above and right) was one of the smallest, carrying only eight passengers. But even the big Boeing 247D took only 10. Fixed rows of seats only became standard in the 1930s; the first passengers rode in loose wicker armchairs. Even in the 1930s, a long plane journey could be quite an ordeal. Without the pressurized cabins of today (p. 34), airliners tended to fly low and passengers were shaken around all over the place by turbulence. If they flew high to avoid the weather, the poor passengers might endure bitter cold and altitude sickness.

Passenger cabin of De Havilland Dragon

Highly reliable 550-hp Pratt and Whitney Wasp air-cooled radial engine

Variable pitch propellers (p. 31) to give both high cruising speed and extra power for takeoff

Tailplane

Electric rams to fold landing gear up into the wing after takeoff

FLYING BOAT TO EGYPT
Big flying boats enabled people to fly vast distances to exotic places. Their ability to land on water was vital when airports were few and far between, mechanical breakdown was a real possibility, and long, slow journeys had to be broken by overnight stops.

Monoplane wing good for economy and speed

Aileron

Powerful electric light for night landing

IMPERIAL STYLE
British Handley Page biplanes, such as this Heracles, were the biggest and most luxurious airliners of the 1930s. They were also very safe, flying more than 2 million miles (3 million km) for Imperial Airways without a fatality. However, they were slow and old-fashioned compared to the American airliners.

Jetliner

THE JET AIRLINER has transformed air travel since the 1950s. Before then, only the wealthy could afford to fly. Today, millions of ordinary people travel by air each year. Jetliners are fast and quiet compared to earlier planes. They can also fly high above the weather, carrying people smoothly in cabins that are pressurized to protect passengers from the reduction in air pressure at this height. In outline, the jets of today look little different from those of 30 years ago, but under the skin, there is a great deal of advanced technology. Sophisticated electronic control and navigation systems have made jetliners much safer to fly in. Airframes now include light, strong carbon-fiber and other "composite" materials, while computer-aided design has made wings more streamlined, reducing fuel costs. And advanced turbofan engines keep engine noise to a minimum.

ARMCHAIRS IN THE SKY
The smoothness of the engines, low cabin noise, and high-altitude flying made jetliners very comfortable.

BIT BY BIT
Modern jetliners are built up from a number of sections, and bolted, riveted, and bonded together with strong adhesive. To keep the number of joints to a minimum, as few sections as possible are used.

Mounting for wing root, containing central fuel tank

FUSELAGE SECTION
The fuselage tube is the same diameter over most of its length. This makes it cheap and easy to construct, because all the frames and tube pieces are the same size and shape. If the manufacturer wants to make the plane longer or shorter, all that has to be done is to add or take away a fuselage section.

Central section of BAe 146 fuselage under construction

Jack placed in the undercarriage recess to support the fuselage during construction

Green chromate-based anticorrosion treatment, prior to painting

Wing skin made from a single piece of metal for extra strength

Cavity for fuel tank

THE WING
As wing design has improved, so the wings of jetliners have become slimmer in comparison to the wings of older airliners (pp. 32–33). This keeps drag to a minimum. Because they cruise at high speeds, jetliner wings also carry a complicated array of flaps and ailerons for extra lift and control at low speeds for takeoff and landing, and spoiler flaps (air brakes) to slow down the plane quickly after landing.

Engine mounting pylon

Mounting for inner flaps or spoilers that flip up to slow down the plane after landing

Hydraulic flap control pipe

DE HAVILLAND COMET

The Comet, the world's first jetliner, entered service in 1952. It halved international flight times, but early Comets were involved in some tragic accidents. Only with the Boeing 707 (1958) and the Douglas DC-8 (1959) did the age of jet travel really begin.

JUMBO JET

When the huge Boeing 747, the first wide-bodied jet, entered service in 1970, many airline experts wondered whether enough passengers could ever be found to fly in it. In fact, the jumbo jet, as it became known, helped to make air travel affordable for billions of people for the first time.

BOEING 787

Called the Dreamliner, the Boeing 787 was due to enter service in 2011. It had a revolutionary new design that used lightweight carbon-fiber for large parts of the main structure. The intention was to reduce weight and make it the most fuel-efficient airliner on the market.

Light, alloy-hoop frame, machined from a single piece of metal for strength

Brackets for overhead luggage lockers

Soundproofing insulation

Aluminum alloy skin

Passenger compartment floor

Electric control wires

Hydraulic control pipes

Stringers bonded along the fuselage skin for extra strength

Luggage hold

Inside a fuselage section of the BAe 146

INSIDE THE FUSELAGE

The structure of a jetliner needs to be immensely strong to withstand the stresses of high-speed flight, and the constant strain of pressurization and depressurization. Any weaknesses could be disastrous. So the strength and durability of every little section is carefully assessed—a huge task that once involved scores of engineers called stressmen but which is now done by computers. Yet strength alone is not enough. The structure must be light, too, which is why aluminum alloy is used extensively. There are hoop frames and stringers all the way down the inside of the fuselage, but these are small and much of the fuselage's strength comes from the metal tube that forms its skin. This makes the structure both light and strong.

Rear view of the right wing of the BAe 146 under construction

Mounting for roll spoiler flap, which stabilizes the plane during banking

Mounting point for large flaps that extend out and down behind the wing for low-speed flight

Aileron

COMPLETED JETLINER

The BAe 146 was a medium-sized jetliner. It was one of the UK's most successful civil designs, with more than 380 being built between 1983 and 2002.

Jet propulsion

THE BIRTH OF THE JET ENGINE in the late 1930s marked a revolution in aviation. Some piston-engined planes were very highly tuned and were flying at speeds in excess of 440 mph (700 kph)—but only by burning a great deal of fuel. Jet engines made speeds like this so easy to achieve that, by the early 1960s, even big airliners on scheduled services were flying faster—and some military jets could streak along at 1,500 mph (2,500 kph), more than twice the speed of sound. Now, almost all airliners, most military planes, and many small business planes (executive jets) are powered by one of the several different kinds of jet engine. With the exception of the Concorde (see opposite), supersonic flight has proved too noisy and expensive for airliners, but jet engine technology is still making steady progress.

PIONEER JET
The first prototype jet engines were built at the same time by Hans von Ohain in Germany and Frank Whittle in Britain—although neither knew of the other's work. Whittle's engine was first used in the Gloster E28/39 of 1941 (above).

BREAKING THE SOUND BARRIER
In 1947, in the specially built Bell X-1 rocket plane, test pilot Chuck Yeager succeeded in flying faster than the speed of sound—about 700 mph (1,100 kph).

Turbine power

Jet engines should really be called gas turbines. Like piston engines, their power comes from burning fuel. The difference is that they burn fuel continuously to spin the blades of a turbine rather than intermittently to push on a piston. In a turbojet, the turbine simply turns the compressor. In a turbofan, it drives the big fan at the front of the engine as well.

Rotating compressor blades draw in air and squeeze it

Fuel sprayed into compressed air burns continuously

Turbine driven around by hot gases

High-speed stream of hot exhaust gases thrusts plane forward

Entrance to engine core

TURBOJET
The simplest jets, called turbojets, work by pushing out a jet of hot exhaust gas. The reaction from this mass of air moving rearward at speed thrusts the plane forward, like a deflating balloon. In turbofan jets, the hot gas jet is combined with the backdraft from a multibladed fan, while in turboprops the plane is driven by a propeller alone.

Cold stream

Giant fan drives some air into the engine core and bypasses some around it

Engine core drives the turbine and provides a little extra thrust

Hot stream

TURBOFAN
The high-speed exhaust stream of a turbojet is fine for ultrafast military planes. The Concorde also used turbojets, but airliners today have quieter, cheaper-to-run turbofans. In these, air driven by a huge fan spun by extra turbines bypasses the engine core, giving a huge boost in thrust at low speeds.

The stream of air bypassing the engine core provides most of the thrust at low speeds

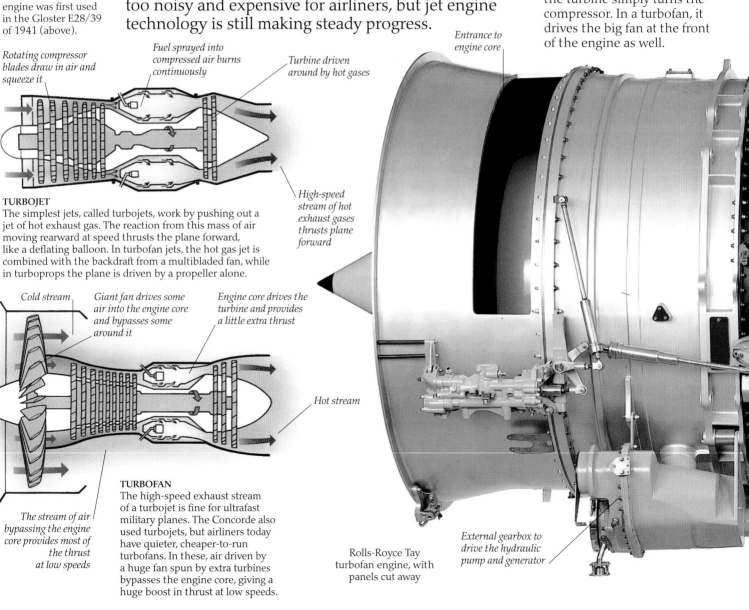

Rolls-Royce Tay turbofan engine, with panels cut away

External gearbox to drive the hydraulic pump and generator

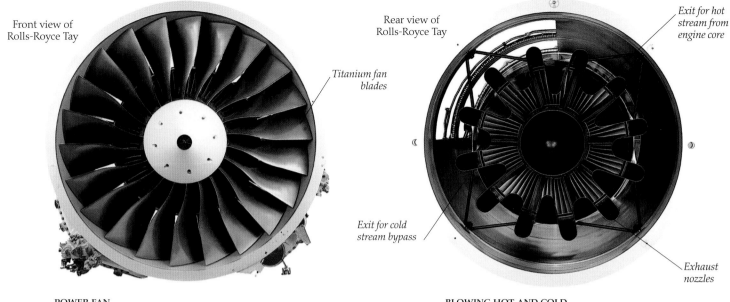

Front view of
Rolls-Royce Tay

*Titanium fan
blades*

Rear view of
Rolls-Royce Tay

*Exit for hot
stream from
engine core*

*Exit for cold
stream bypass*

*Exhaust
nozzles*

POWER FAN
A modern turbofan engine owes much of its immense
power to the giant fan at the front, and the design of
the fan blades has a critical effect on fuel economy.
In the Rolls-Royce Tay, the fan pushes more than three
times as much air through the bypass duct to provide
propulsion as through the engine core. In earlier
turbofans, the proportions were about equal.

*Combustion
chamber where
fuel spray burns
continuously in
the compressed air*

BLOWING HOT AND COLD
Most of the turbofan's propulsive power is
provided by the cold stream of air that rushes
through the bypass duct. The faster, hot-stream
gas from the engine shoots out through the
lobed exhaust nozzles. The lobes help mix the
hot and cold streams quickly and reduce noise.

*Bypass casing made of
carbon fiber and plastic
honeycomb for lightness
and sound insulation*

*Turbines made
of exotic metal
alloys to endure
running very hot
all the time*

BEYOND SOUND
The only successful
supersonic airliner,
the Concorde was in
service from 1976
until 2003. It flew
the Atlantic at
twice the speed of
conventional jets.
However, its
turbojet engines
proved very noisy
and its flying costs
were extremely high.

*Rows of rotating
compressor blades drive
air through the engine,
compressing the air as
it passes through*

The
Concorde

Landing gear

T HE FIRST AIRPLANES landed on wheels borrowed from
motorcycles and cars, mounted on wooden or metal struts.
These wheels did the job, but the shock of a poor landing
was often enough to make the struts collapse. Soon the
undercarriage, as it became known, was given basic springs to
cushion the blow and special aviation wheels were designed.
As planes grew heavier and landing and takeoff speeds rose,
wooden struts and wire wheels gave way to pressed-steel
wheels and strong, fluid-damped landing legs. Wheels were
also mounted farther apart on the wings for extra stability.
From the 1940s on, wheels on all but the smallest, slowest
planes were folded up into the wings in flight to reduce air
resistance. With the coming of the jet age after World War II,
the demands on landing gear increased still further. It was on
jetliner landing gear that innovations later adopted on cars,
such as disc and antilock brakes, were first tried. Modern
jetliner undercarriages are highly sophisticated pieces of
machinery, with elaborate suspension and braking systems.
They are designed to support a 150-ton plane landing
at 125 mph (200 kph) or more and to
bring it quickly and
safely to a halt.

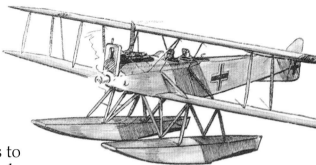

LANDING ON WATER
In the days when good landing strips were few and
far between, it made sense to land on water. On
seaplanes, a step two-thirds along the underside of
the float helped it skim over the water's surface like
a speedboat. This reduced water drag enough for
the aircraft to reach takeoff speed.

LIGHTLY SPOKED
There were no brakes on this wheel from a
pre-World War I plane. Because of this, it did
not need elaborate crisscrossed spokes to
resist braking forces.

*Wooden
landing
strut*

*Skid to keep
the plane from
tipping forward
when landing on
soft ground*

*Shock
absorbers of
elasticated-rubber*

SPRUNG TAIL-SKID
The rear ends of the
pioneers' planes were so
light that there was no
need for a wheel; a simple
skid was sufficient.

COMING DOWN GENTLY
The 1909 Deperdussin came
down so lightly and slowly that
elasticated rubber straps made fairly
effective landing springs. Curved
skids on the front helped to stop
the plane from pitching forward
when landing on soft ground—a
common hazard in the early days.

LANDING LIGHT

As landing speeds rose sharply with the coming of jets in the 1950s, ever longer, paved runways had to be built for jetliners to land safely. Bigger aircraft also switched from single-wheel to multiwheel (bogie) landing legs. Bogies were not only smaller and lighter, but also spread the landing load over a wider area and reduced the danger from a burst tire. At the same time, most planes acquired wheels under the nose. Nose wheels meant that planes could land level and, in effect, drive on to the runway like a car. Before nose wheels, pilots had to skillfully stall the plane just above the ground, letting the main and tail wheels drop on to the runway at the same time.

UP AND UNDER

In the bid for speed, World War II fighters such as the Spitfire (above) pioneered simple mechanisms for folding the wheels right up into the wings during flight.

Hydraulic disc-brake pipes

"Liquid" spring and shock absorber to absorb main landing shocks

SPITFIRE WHEEL

Light and robust cast-alloy wheels, now common on cars, were used on aircraft like the Spitfire many years before they were tried on cars.

Hydraulic ram slides up inside main leg to absorb landing shocks

Auxiliary shock absorber

Swivel joints to allow for spring compression

STEEL WHEEL

Pressed-steel wheels provided the extra strength needed for the faster, heavier planes of the 1920s. This one is from a Hawker Hart similar to that on page 24.

TWO BIG WHEELS

The big monoplane airliners and bombers of the 1930s and 1940s had a huge retracting wheel on each wing. On this 1930s Armstrong-Whitworth airliner, the rear landing leg folded in the middle so that a hydraulic jack could lift the wheel back up into the engine housing in flight.

Bogie with four twin-tired wheels

Tires designed to stand enormous loads and huge heat buildup on landing

Landing leg from 1950s Avro Vulcan bomber

Controlling the plane

A CAR OR A BOAT can only be steered to the left or right, but an airplane can be controlled in three dimensions. It can pitch nose-up or nose-down to climb or dive. It can roll from side to side, dipping one wing or the other. And it can yaw to the left or to the right, like a car steering. For many in-flight maneuvers, the pilot has to use not just one control, but all three simultaneously—which is why flying demands good coordination. Indeed, all the time the plane is in the air, the pilot must constantly trim the controls simply to keep the plane flying straight and level—for even on the calmest day, there is air turbulence to tip it off balance. Devices called automatic pilots compensate for such upsets and make life for the pilot much easier.

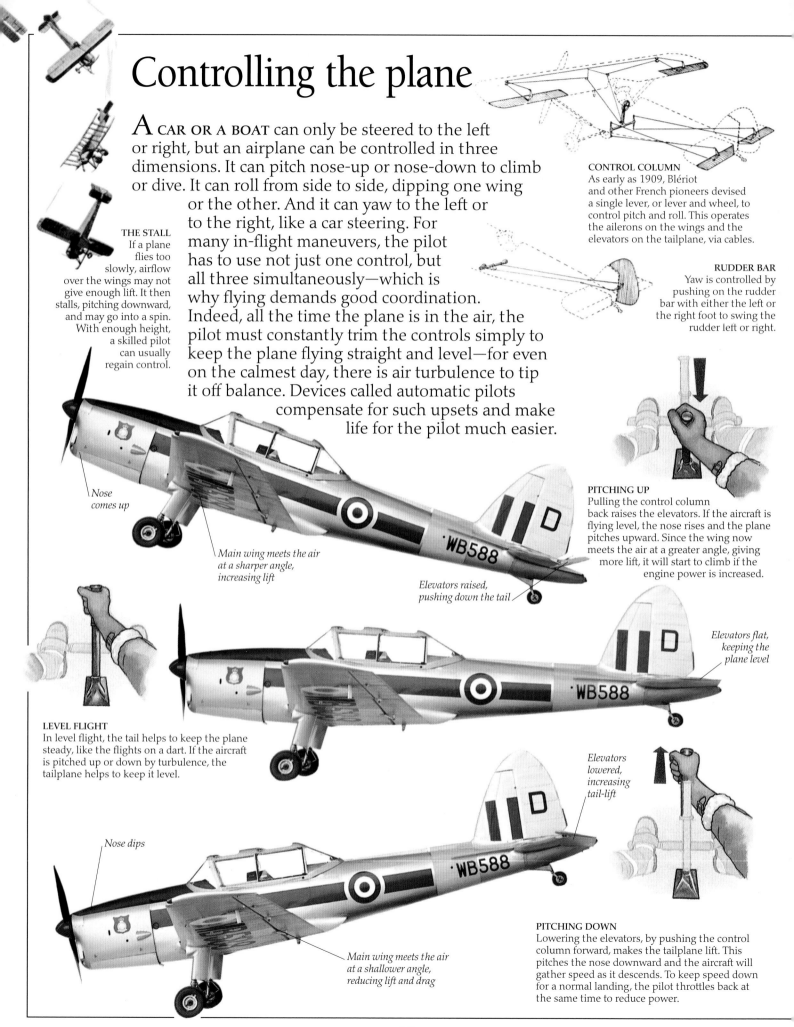

CONTROL COLUMN
As early as 1909, Blériot and other French pioneers devised a single lever, or lever and wheel, to control pitch and roll. This operates the ailerons on the wings and the elevators on the tailplane, via cables.

RUDDER BAR
Yaw is controlled by pushing on the rudder bar with either the left or the right foot to swing the rudder left or right.

THE STALL
If a plane flies too slowly, airflow over the wings may not give enough lift. It then stalls, pitching downward, and may go into a spin. With enough height, a skilled pilot can usually regain control.

Nose comes up

Main wing meets the air at a sharper angle, increasing lift

Elevators raised, pushing down the tail

PITCHING UP
Pulling the control column back raises the elevators. If the aircraft is flying level, the nose rises and the plane pitches upward. Since the wing now meets the air at a greater angle, giving more lift, it will start to climb if the engine power is increased.

Elevators flat, keeping the plane level

LEVEL FLIGHT
In level flight, the tail helps to keep the plane steady, like the flights on a dart. If the aircraft is pitched up or down by turbulence, the tailplane helps to keep it level.

Elevators lowered, increasing tail-lift

Nose dips

Main wing meets the air at a shallower angle, reducing lift and drag

PITCHING DOWN
Lowering the elevators, by pushing the control column forward, makes the tailplane lift. This pitches the nose downward and the aircraft will gather speed as it descends. To keep speed down for a normal landing, the pilot throttles back at the same time to reduce power.

ROLLING LEFT

To roll to the left, the pilot pushes the control column over to the left. This raises the aileron on the left wing, reducing lift, and lowers the aileron on the right wing, increasing lift.

Left aileron raised, reducing lift on left wing

Right aileron lowered, increasing lift on right wing

ROLLING RIGHT

To roll to the right, the pilot pushes the control column to the right, raising the right aileron and lowering the left aileron. If the ailerons are kept deflected, the plane will roll farther and farther and eventually roll all the way over. So, once the plane is rolled at the right angle, the pilot must straighten the column again.

Left aileron lowered, increasing lift on left wing

Right aileron raised, reducing lift on right wing

TURNING LEFT

While moving on the ground, pushing with the left foot on the rudder bar will swing the rudder over to the left and make the plane yaw around the same way. But a plane cannot be turned like this in the air. Instead, it has to be banked around—like cornering on a bicycle. To make a banked turn, the pilot has to yaw and roll the plane at the same time. Banking for a left turn means pushing the control column to the left while pressing on the rudder with the left foot.

Rudder swung left, yawing the plane to the left

TURNING RIGHT

Banking for a right turn means pressing on the rudder bar with the right foot, while pushing the control column over to the right at the same time. Balancing the rudder and control column movement to achieve just the right bank angle requires skill and experience.

Rudder swung right, yawing the plane to the right

AERIAL TWISTS

Almost from the first, pilots started trying new maneuvers, and in many air forces, aerobatics is part of routine training. In the 1920s, "flying circuses" thrilled audiences all over the world with their breathtaking aerobatic displays in agile biplanes.

In the cockpit

Control wheel pivoted backward and forward for diving and climbing, just like a control stick

CLOSED-IN COCKPITS had to await the development of safety glass in the late 1920s. Up until then, pilots sat in the open, exposed to howling winds, freezing cold, and damp—with nothing more to protect them than a tiny windshield and warm clothes. Naturally, comfort was a low priority in these open cockpits, and they were very basic and functional in appearance. There were few instruments, and engine gauges were just as often on the engine itself as in the cockpit. The layout of the main flight controls became established fairly early on, with a rudder bar at the pilot's feet for turning, and a control column known as a joystick between the knees for diving, climbing, and banking. Some early planes had a wheel rather than a joystick, but it served the same purpose. This basic layout is still used in light planes today.

DEPERDUSSIN 1909
The cockpits of the earliest planes were very simple, for they had no instruments. With a large fuel tank obscuring the view ahead, the pilot had to lean out of the cockpit constantly to check altitude and pitch.

VICKERS VIMY 1919
The Vimy was designed toward the end of World War I for long-range British bombing raids over industrial targets in Germany, and the cockpit was laid out accordingly, with two seats—one for the pilot and one for the observer. The pilot had to read engine speed and oil pressure from gauges mounted on the engines themselves.

Clock

Altimeter to show height

ATLANTIC FLIGHT *above*
The Vimy was the plane in which John Alcock and Arthur Brown made the first nonstop flight over the Atlantic on June 14–15, 1919, enduring 16 hours of freezing fog and drizzle in an open cockpit.

Hand-wound magnet to provide electric current for starting

Instrument light switches

Inclinometers to show bank and pitch

Compass

Engine radiator shutter control

Rudder bar

Control wheel turned to bank left or right

Engine throttle and fuel mixture control

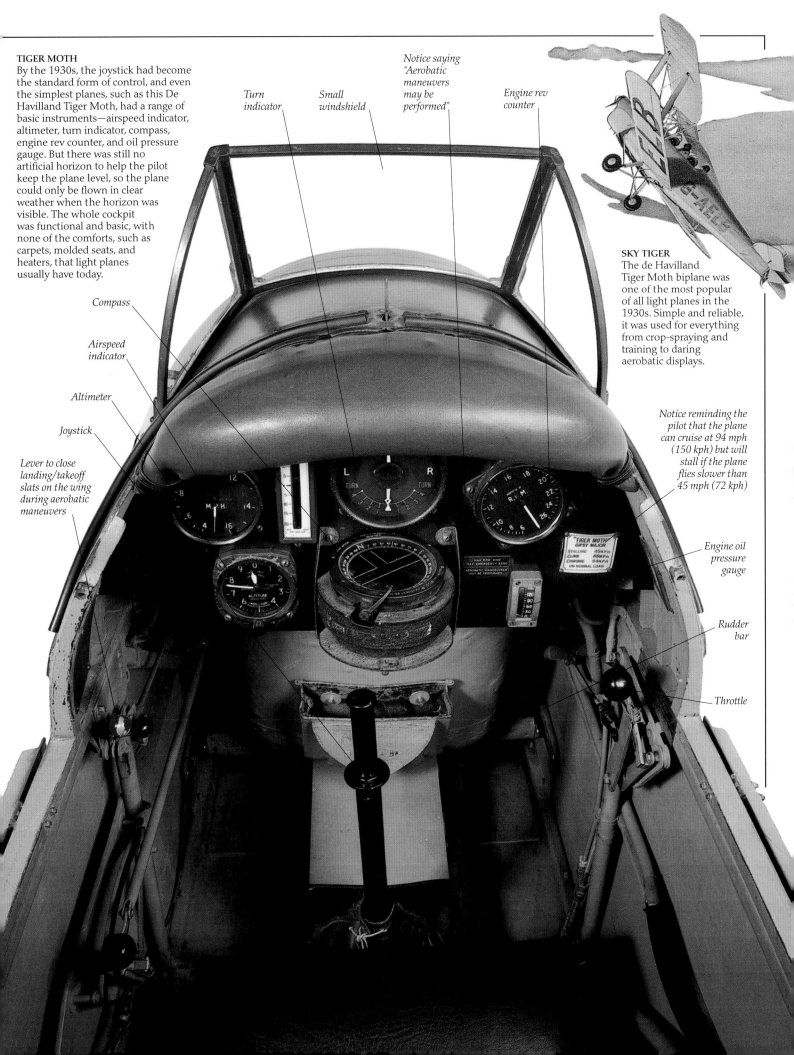

TIGER MOTH
By the 1930s, the joystick had become the standard form of control, and even the simplest planes, such as this De Havilland Tiger Moth, had a range of basic instruments—airspeed indicator, altimeter, turn indicator, compass, engine rev counter, and oil pressure gauge. But there was still no artificial horizon to help the pilot keep the plane level, so the plane could only be flown in clear weather when the horizon was visible. The whole cockpit was functional and basic, with none of the comforts, such as carpets, molded seats, and heaters, that light planes usually have today.

Compass

Airspeed indicator

Altimeter

Joystick

Lever to close landing/takeoff slats on the wing during aerobatic maneuvers

Turn indicator

Small windshield

Notice saying "Aerobatic maneuvers may be performed"

Engine rev counter

SKY TIGER
The de Havilland Tiger Moth biplane was one of the most popular of all light planes in the 1930s. Simple and reliable, it was used for everything from crop-spraying and training to daring aerobatic displays.

Notice reminding the pilot that the plane can cruise at 94 mph (150 kph) but will stall if the plane flies slower than 45 mph (72 kph)

Engine oil pressure gauge

Rudder bar

Throttle

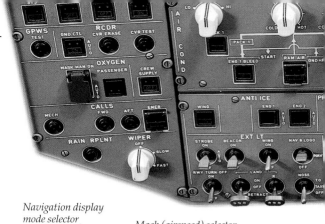

On the flight deck

THE FLIGHT DECK OF A MODERN JETLINER looks dauntingly complicated, with its array of switches and electronic displays for things such as engine condition, hydraulics, and navigational aids, not to mention the basic flight controls. Today, computers have taken over many functions, and the dials of older aircraft have largely been replaced by neat screens on which the pilot can change the data displayed with the flick of a switch.

Navigation display mode selector

Mach (airspeed) selector

Navigational display in plan mode

Primary flight display

Flight deck simulator of an Airbus A320 jetliner

Standby airspeed indicator

Standby altimeter

Standby artificial horizon

Digital distance and radio magnetic indicator (DDRMI)

Systems data display

Glass cockpit

Most of the information in this cockpit comes up on screens, not dials, which is why it is known as a glass cockpit. The two most important screens are the primary flight display (which simultaneously shows data from all the flight instruments) and the navigational display (which combines the functions of compass, radar screen, and map).

Captain's side

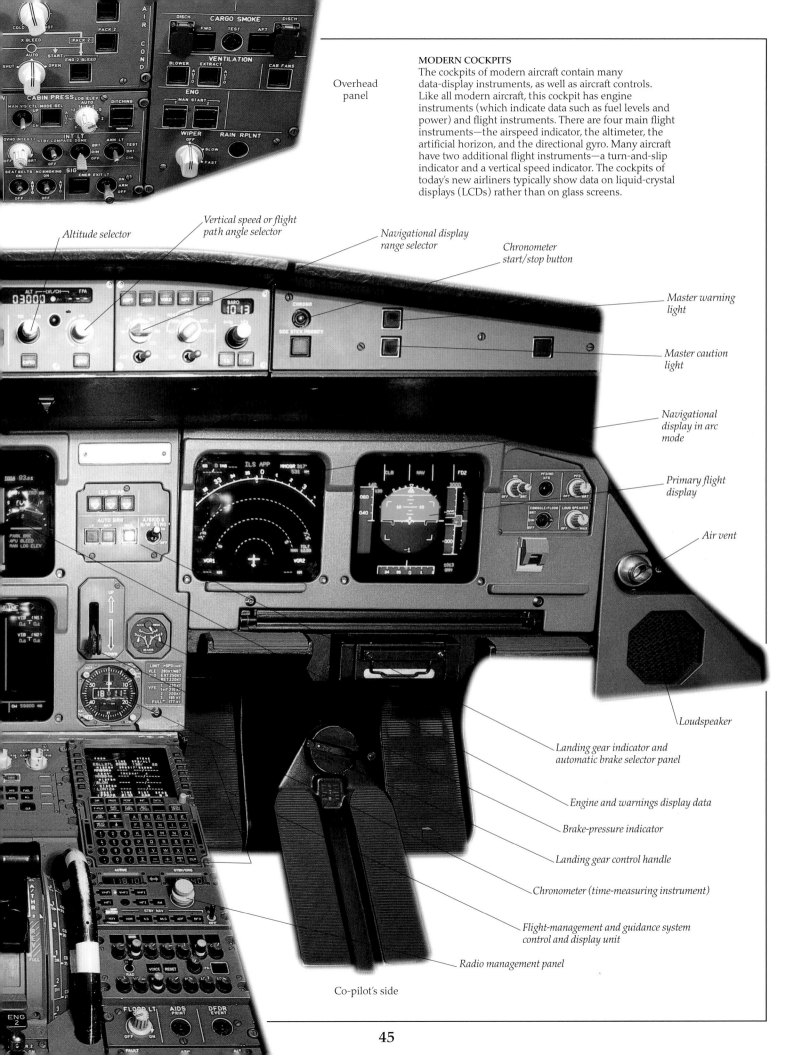

Overhead panel

MODERN COCKPITS

The cockpits of modern aircraft contain many data-display instruments, as well as aircraft controls. Like all modern aircraft, this cockpit has engine instruments (which indicate data such as fuel levels and power) and flight instruments. There are four main flight instruments—the airspeed indicator, the altimeter, the artificial horizon, and the directional gyro. Many aircraft have two additional flight instruments—a turn-and-slip indicator and a vertical speed indicator. The cockpits of today's new airliners typically show data on liquid-crystal displays (LCDs) rather than on glass screens.

Altitude selector

Vertical speed or flight path angle selector

Navigational display range selector

Chronometer start/stop button

Master warning light

Master caution light

Navigational display in arc mode

Primary flight display

Air vent

Loudspeaker

Landing gear indicator and automatic brake selector panel

Engine and warnings display data

Brake-pressure indicator

Landing gear control handle

Chronometer (time-measuring instrument)

Flight-management and guidance system control and display unit

Radio management panel

Co-pilot's side

Flying instruments

THE WRIGHT BROTHERS (p. 14) flew with nothing more in the way of instruments than an engine rev counter, a stopwatch, and a wind meter to tell them roughly how fast the plane was going. But the dangers of stalling by flying too slow soon made it clear that every flying machine should have an accurate airspeed indicator as standard. As aircraft began to fly higher and farther, an altimeter to indicate height and a magnetic compass to help keep a straight course were quickly added. Yet for a long time, pilots flew "by the seat of their pants," judging the plane's attitude by feel alone when they could not see. It was only with Elmer Sperry's development of gyroscope-stabilized instruments in 1929 that pilots were given a bank-and-turn indicator and an artificial horizon. Gyroscopes—a kind of spinning top that stays level no matter what angle the plane is at—enabled them to "fly on instruments" when visibility was poor.

Pressure plate

Spring

DOUBLE TUBE
This is one of the first instruments to give a continuous and reliable indication of airspeed. It works by comparing static pressure (ordinary air pressure) with dynamic pressure (from the plane pushing forward). Its twin pipes point into the airflow, one running straight through but the other ending in a perforated cylinder. The pressure difference between the two, measured by a flexible diaphragm, indicates the airspeed.

Farnborough airspeed indicator c. 1909

Diaphragm

HOW FAST?
Among the earliest speed indicators were anemometers (wind meters) adapted from weather forecasting. The pilot got a rough idea of how fast the plane was going by timing so many seconds on a stopwatch while noting on the meter dials how many times the airflow turned the fan on the front.

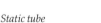

Static pipe   *Dynamic pipe*

Static tube   *Pitot head*

Dynamic tube

Connecting tube

MACH METER
As jet planes approached and even exceeded the speed of sound in the 1950s, they were given Mach meters. These showed how fast the plane was flying relative to the speed of sound.

MACH .8 .9 .6 1.0 .5

PITOT HEAD
The twin-tube pressure method pioneered by Farnborough soon became the basis for measuring airspeed on all aircraft. The twin tube was refined into the pressure-sensing pitot head mounted on the airframe. Rubber tubes connected the pitot to the airspeed gauge in the cockpit.

Gauge

AIR SPEED

Ogilvie airspeed indicator c. 1918

20 40 KNOTS 10 60 5

SPEED LIMIT
In the years after World War II, airspeed indicators often had a pointer (arrow head) showing the maximum safe speed of the plane.

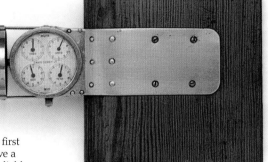

WING SPRING

This simple device dates from 1910, but even in the 1930s some planes still used them. Wing springs showed airspeed according to how far the pressure plate was forced back against a spring by the airflow.

HOW STRAIGHT?

In this bank-and-turn indicator, a simple spirit level shows how much the plane is banking. Directional changes are indicated by the upper turn needle, which is linked to an electrically driven gyroscope.

WHICH WAY?

Landing in poor weather was made much safer by this gyroscopic instrument. It helped the pilot maintain a course and glide slope set by a radio beam that lined up with the runway.

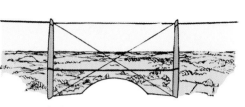

With the sighting string below the horizon, the plane is diving.

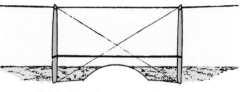

With the sighting string above the horizon, the plane is climbing.

HOW HIGH?

To tell how high they were, the pioneer aviators used to whip from their pockets little altimeters such as the Elliott (below)—similar to those used by mountaineers for years before. But the aerial antics of World War I fighters showed the need for a big dial fixed to the panel (left).

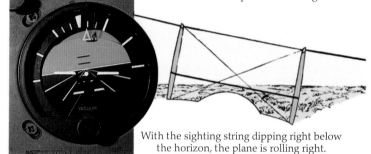

With the sighting string dipping right below the horizon, the plane is rolling right.

HOW LEVEL?

In the early days, pilots could only look at the horizon, perhaps with the aid of a sighting string (above right), to tell them how much their machine was pitching or rolling. At night, or in thick cloud, the pilot would soon be completely disorientated. Research showed that even the most experienced pilot could not fly "blind" for more than eight minutes without getting into a spin. The answer was a gyroscopic artificial horizon.

Inside a black box

All modern airliners and military planes now carry a "black box," or flight data recorder, to give a complete history of the flight in case of an accident. The box, which is not necessarily black, is connected up to all the aircraft's main systems and records everything that happens to it during the flight, monitoring flight deck instruments, engine data, and even what the crew says.

BOXED IN

All the flight data in this 1990 box was stored on magnetic tape. An incredibly strong, well-insulated case of titanium alloy protected the tape against crash damage and fire. Today, black boxes record data onto memory chips like those in a computer. They still have a tough, protective casing.

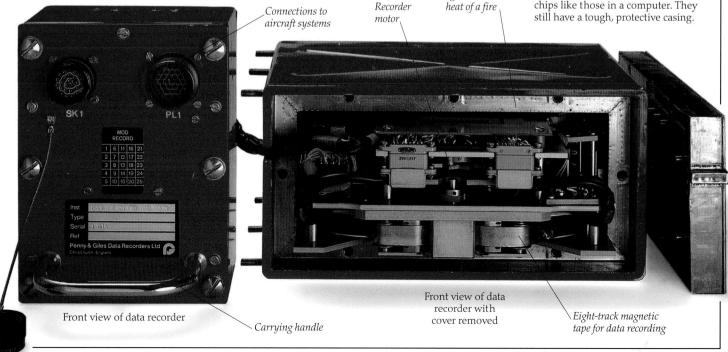

Connections to aircraft systems

Recorder motor

Kevlar lining to insulate the recorder against the heat of a fire

Front view of data recorder

Carrying handle

Front view of data recorder with cover removed

Eight-track magnetic tape for data recording

Rotating wings

THE IDEA OF FLYING on rotating wings is old. As long ago as 1400, European children played with flying toys with whirring blades. Indeed, up until the Wright brothers' *Flyer*, many felt the future of flight lay with rotating rather than fixed wings. Spinning wings, they knew, would slice through the air to provide lift just like fixed wings (p. 11). But while a fixed wing plane must keep moving, a rotating wing plane could hover in one place. In the early 1900s, many whirling wing contraptions did rise off the ground. Yet the chances of controlled flight seemed remote until a Spaniard, Juan de la Cierva, created the autogiro.

JUAN DE LA CIERVA
Cierva was obsessed from an early age with the idea of building a rotary-wing aircraft that would make flying safer.

Rotor blade

LOOK—NO WINGS!
The autogiro was never meant to be a helicopter. It was designed as a wingless plane that would be safer than fixed-wing aircraft because it would not stall simply by flying too slow. Indeed, Cierva's first autogiros did have stubby wings to assist takeoff (right). Publicity for the autogiro always emphasized how it could drift safely to the ground "slower than a parachute," in case of engine failure.

Autogiro

In early helicopter experiments, inventors had used ever more powerful engines to get their machines to rise. Cierva's stroke of genius was to see that rotating wings can provide lift without the engine. Like a maple pod whirling gently down to Earth, a freely rotating wing continues to spin by itself when moving through the air, pushed around by the pressure of air on the underside of the wings. He called this self-rotation, or autogiro.

K4232

CIERVA C-30
The C-30 was the most successful of all the autogiros made in the 1930s. This example is one of many sold to the military for reconnaissance and using as markers to set up radars in World War II.

Unique upswept tailplane with normal camber on this side only to counterbalance the rotation of the blades

Fabric-covered steel-tube fuselage similar to that of a biplane

Steerable tail-wheel

CARS OF THE SKY
For a while in the 1930s, many believed that autogiros would be the Model T Fords of the air—aircraft for everyone that would do away with traffic jams once and for all. Ads for the Pitcairn company, which made autogiros in the US, were aimed clearly at the fashionable set. What could be simpler, they suggested, than to jump into the autogiro on your front lawn and drop in at your country club for a quick game of golf?

PIVOTING BLADES
Primitive rotor craft tended to roll over because the advancing blade cut through the air faster than the receding one, and so was lifted more. Cierva solved this problem with hinges that allowed the advancing blade to rise without affecting the plane.

Blade lift hinge

Sideways drag-hinges and shock absorbers allow the blades to advance or trail slightly as they rotate, reducing the stress on the root of each blade

Hanging control column to allow the pilot to tilt the blades in any direction

Drive from the engine to start the rotors spinning for takeoff

SNAIL'S FLIGHT
To demonstrate its safety potential, the C-30 would fly into the wind so slowly that it could be outpaced by a runner.

Rotor blade construction, showing how similar the profile is to conventional wings

150-hp Armstrong Siddeley seven-cylinder radial engine

Conventional propeller to pull the aircraft forward for takeoff and normal flight

Soft, oil-filled shock absorbers to absorb landing shocks

Helicopter

Rotor blades

Of all flying machines, none is quite so versatile as the helicopter. Its whirling rotor blades enable it to shoot straight up in the air, hover for minute after minute, and land on an area little bigger than that taken up by a bus. It burns up fuel at a frightening rate because the engine, via the rotors, provides all the lifting force. It also takes great skill to fly, for the pilot has three flight controls to handle—rudder, collective pitch, and cyclic pitch— one more than the conventional aircraft (pp. 40–41). But the helicopter has proved its worth in many situations, from traffic monitoring to dramatic rescues from sinking ships.

SPINNING DREAMS
Helicopters have a long history, but many early experimenters were regarded as nutcases—perhaps some of them were!

How a helicopter flies

A helicopter's rotor blades are actually long, thin wings. The engine spins them around so that they cut through the air just like a conventional wing (p. 11). In a way, the rotor is also like a huge propeller, hauling the helicopter upward just like a propeller pulling a plane along (p. 30).

Climbing

Hovering

Descending

THE TAIL-ROTOR
Without a tail-rotor, a helicopter would spin around in the opposite way to the rotor blades. The tail-rotor acts like a propeller to resist this effect, which is called torque reaction. The tail-rotor is also a kind of rudder, and the pilot changes the pitch on its blades to swing the tail to the left or right.

Pitch controls

Instrument panel

Swashplate

UP, DOWN, AND HOVERING
To go up or down, the pilot uses the collective pitch control to alter the angle, or pitch, of the rotor blades. When the blades cut through the air almost flat, they give no lift and the helicopter sinks. To climb, the pilot must steepen the pitch of the blades, increasing lift. To hover, however, the pilot must set the blades to a precise angle in between. It all works through a sliding collar on the rotor shaft called the swashplate, which pushes up or pulls down on rods linked to the blades.

TO AND FRO
To fly forward or backward, or to bank for a turn, the pilot tilts the whole rotor with the cyclic pitch control. This tilts the swashplate so that the pitch of each blade varies in turn as it goes around. At the point where the plate is lowest, pitch is shallow and lift is limited. Straight opposite, however, the plate is at its highest and a steep pitch gives a lot of lift. The effect is to tilt the whole rotor over in the way the pilot wants to go, pulling the helicopter with it.

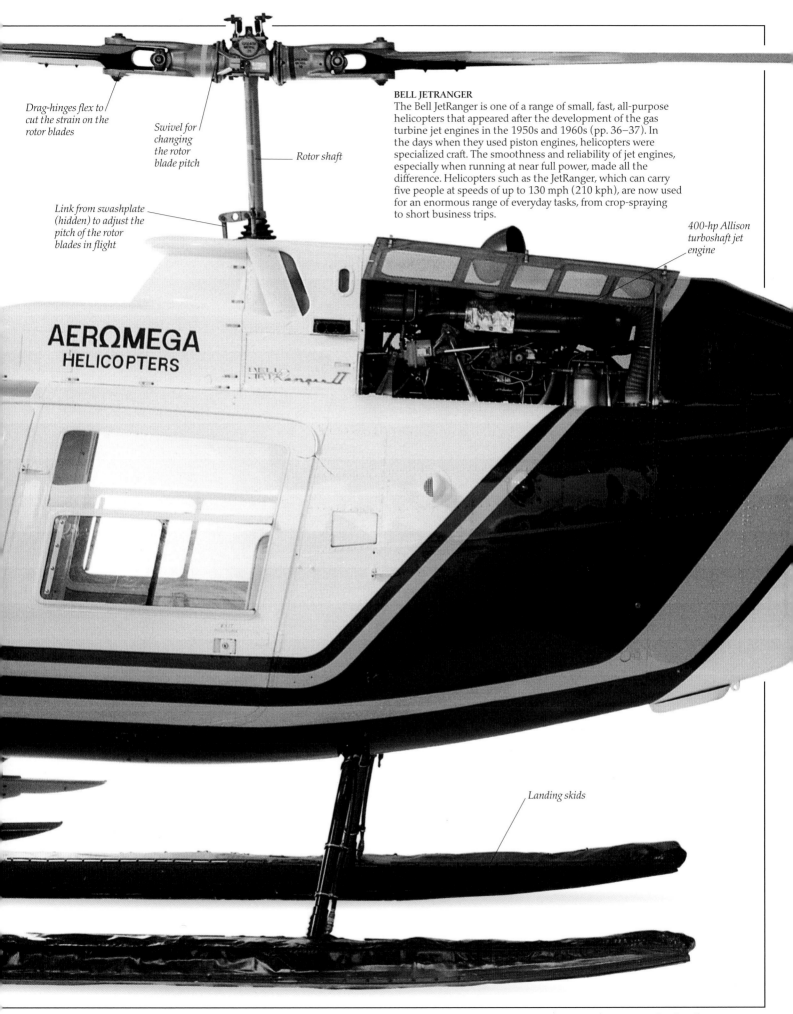

Drag-hinges flex to cut the strain on the rotor blades

Swivel for changing the rotor blade pitch

Rotor shaft

Link from swashplate (hidden) to adjust the pitch of the rotor blades in flight

BELL JETRANGER
The Bell JetRanger is one of a range of small, fast, all-purpose helicopters that appeared after the development of the gas turbine jet engines in the 1950s and 1960s (pp. 36–37). In the days when they used piston engines, helicopters were specialized craft. The smoothness and reliability of jet engines, especially when running at near full power, made all the difference. Helicopters such as the JetRanger, which can carry five people at speeds of up to 130 mph (210 kph), are now used for an enormous range of everyday tasks, from crop-spraying to short business trips.

400-hp Allison turboshaft jet engine

AERΩMEGA HELICOPTERS

Landing skids

Continued on next page

CLIPPER OF THE CLOUDS
The idea of rotary-wing flight fired the imagination of many creative minds in the 19th century. The flying helicopter toys of George Cayley (p. 10) were famous, but many other people built working models. These models did little more than climb up erratically into the air then drop. But the visionary French inventor Gabriel de la Landelle was convinced that one day machines such as the Steam Airliner he drew in 1863 (left) would sail majestically through the sky.

THE FIRST HELICOPTER FLIGHT?
Even in the early 20th century, many people believed helicopters might still beat fixed wing planes into the air. They were wrong. Yet in 1907, just four years after the Wright brothers' first flight, this primitive tandem-rotor helicopter, built by French mechanic Paul Cornu, lifted him clear of the ground, if only for 20 seconds.

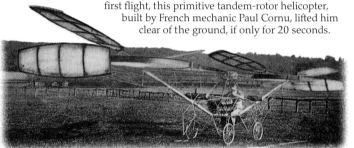

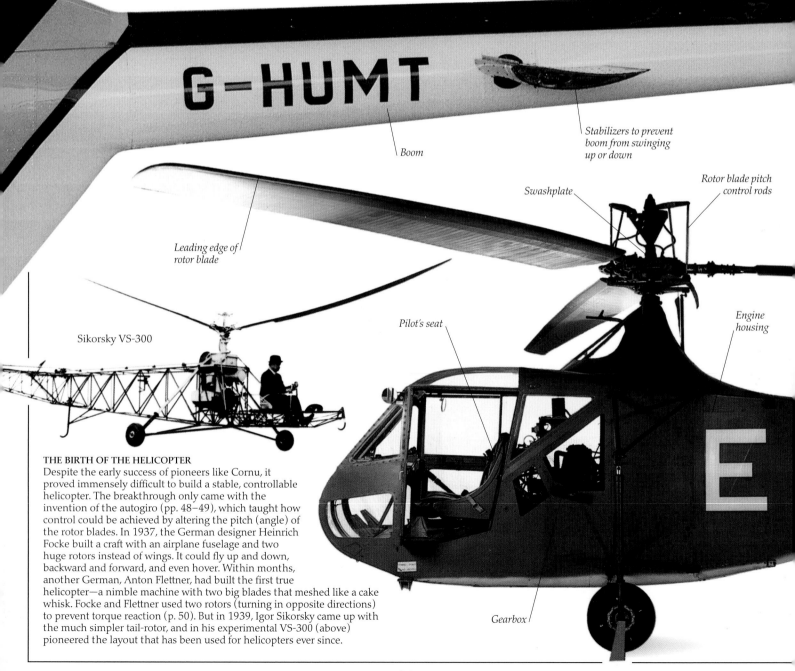

G-HUMT

Boom

Stabilizers to prevent boom from swinging up or down

Swashplate

Rotor blade pitch control rods

Leading edge of rotor blade

Pilot's seat

Engine housing

Sikorsky VS-300

E

THE BIRTH OF THE HELICOPTER
Despite the early success of pioneers like Cornu, it proved immensely difficult to build a stable, controllable helicopter. The breakthrough only came with the invention of the autogiro (pp. 48–49), which taught how control could be achieved by altering the pitch (angle) of the rotor blades. In 1937, the German designer Heinrich Focke built a craft with an airplane fuselage and two huge rotors instead of wings. It could fly up and down, backward and forward, and even hover. Within months, another German, Anton Flettner, had built the first true helicopter—a nimble machine with two big blades that meshed like a cake whisk. Focke and Flettner used two rotors (turning in opposite directions) to prevent torque reaction (p. 50). But in 1939, Igor Sikorsky came up with the much simpler tail-rotor, and in his experimental VS-300 (above) pioneered the layout that has been used for helicopters ever since.

Gearbox

BUTTERFLY WINGS
In the 1870s, the rubber-band-powered helicopter toys made by Alphonse Pénaud and a colleague by the name of Dandrieux were the inspiration for many rotary wing enthusiasts.

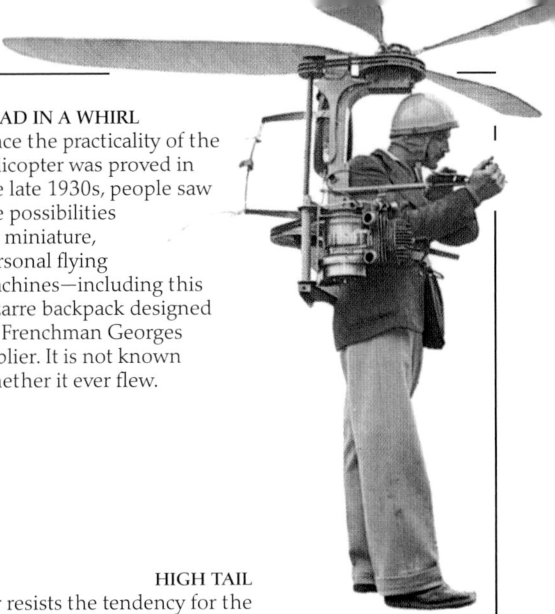

Tail fin

HEAD IN A WHIRL
Once the practicality of the helicopter was proved in the late 1930s, people saw the possibilities for miniature, personal flying machines—including this bizarre backpack designed by Frenchman Georges Sablier. It is not known whether it ever flew.

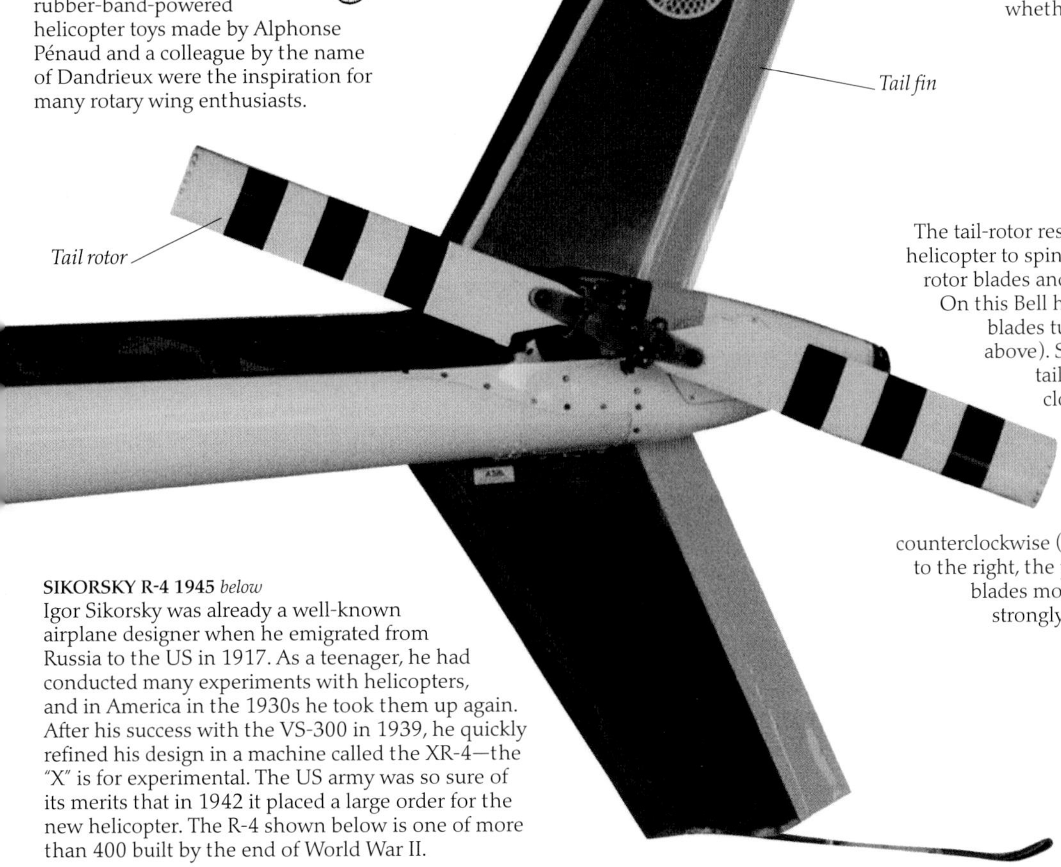

Tail rotor

HIGH TAIL
The tail-rotor resists the tendency for the helicopter to spin round in reaction to the rotor blades and acts as a rudder (p. 50). On this Bell helicopter, the main rotor blades turn clockwise (seen from above). So, to keep it straight, the tail-rotor must push the tail clockwise (toward you). To steer it to the left, the pilot flattens the tail rotor blades so that they push weakly and allow the tail to swing counterclockwise (away from you). To steer to the right, the pilot angles the tail-rotor blades more sharply to pull the tail strongly clockwise (toward you).

SIKORSKY R-4 1945 *below*
Igor Sikorsky was already a well-known airplane designer when he emigrated from Russia to the US in 1917. As a teenager, he had conducted many experiments with helicopters, and in America in the 1930s he took them up again. After his success with the VS-300 in 1939, he quickly refined his design in a machine called the XR-4—the "X" is for experimental. The US army was so sure of its merits that in 1942 it placed a large order for the new helicopter. The R-4 shown below is one of more than 400 built by the end of World War II.

Tail-rotor pitch control wires

Boom

MILITARY USE
The helicopter's ability to reach inaccessible places is invaluable in war.

British Royal Air Force Sikorsky R-4

KK995

Rear landing wheel

Hot-air balloon

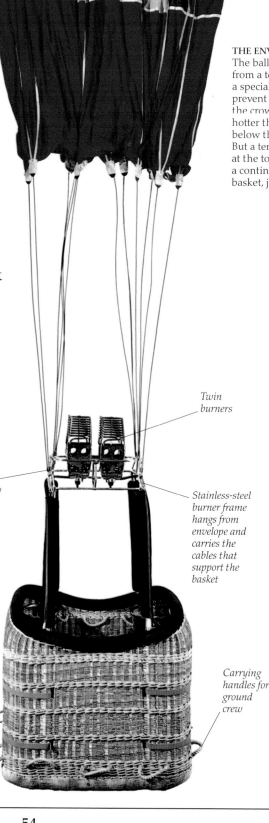

As a sport, ballooning all but died out after World War I—mainly because the gas to fill the balloons had become too difficult and costly to obtain. Then in the 1960s, Ed Yost, Tracy Barnes, and others in the US started to experiment with balloons inflated with hot air, just like the Montgolfier brothers' balloon nearly 200 years earlier. What was new about their balloons was that the envelopes were made of polyurethane-coated nylon, and they were filled by burning liquid propane gas. So successful was the combination that it sparked off a remarkable revival of interest in hot-air ballooning. Today, there are regular hot-air balloon events all over the world, as well as many attempts to break long-distance records.

Light nylon-weave envelope

Envelope assembled by sewing together separate panels of material cut to a pattern

THE ENVELOPE
The balloon's envelope is made from a tough nylon material with a special crisscross weave to prevent it from tearing. Normally, the crown of the balloon gets no hotter than 248°F (120°C), well below the melting-point of nylon. But a temperature sensor is fitted at the top of the envelope, giving a continuous read-out in the basket, just in case.

DIFFERENT SHAPES
With the hot-air balloon revival, modern materials allowed balloon-makers to break away from the traditional balloon shape. At first, they made simple shapes such as drink cans and bottles. Today, you may see a complete French château or two-humped camels floating gently through the sky.

Uncle Sam balloon

Cables end in quick-release spring clips for easy assembly and dismantling

Twin burners

Stainless-steel burner frame hangs from envelope and carries the cables that support the basket

BURNER SUPPORTS
Nylon rods ensure that the gas burners are supported high above the flyers' heads—although in flight, the burners hang from the balloon cables. The gas pipes are strapped to the rods, and a padded protective cover is zipped around them.

Carrying handles for ground crew

INFLATION
Filling the balloon is perhaps the trickiest part of the entire balloon flight. Here, the burner is being used to inflate the balloon on the ground.

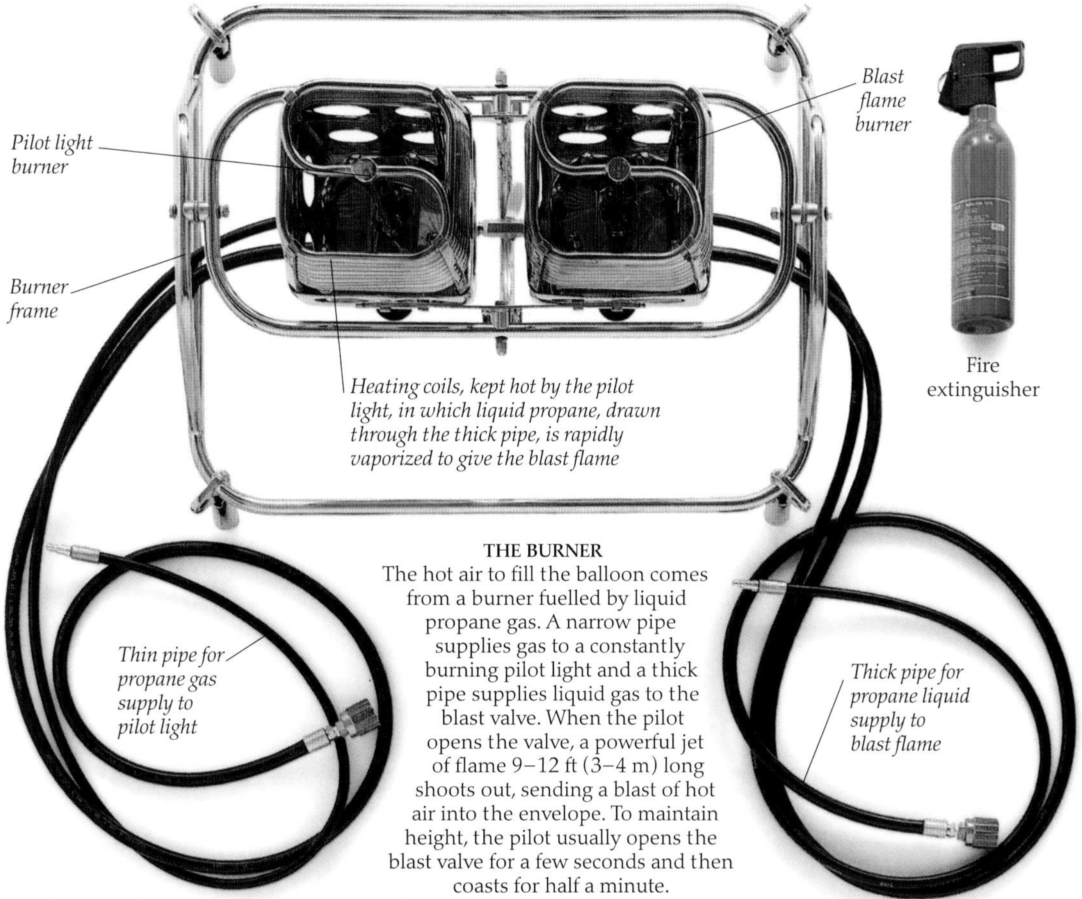

Pilot light burner

Blast flame burner

Burner frame

Heating coils, kept hot by the pilot light, in which liquid propane, drawn through the thick pipe, is rapidly vaporized to give the blast flame

Fire extinguisher

THE BURNER
The hot air to fill the balloon comes from a burner fuelled by liquid propane gas. A narrow pipe supplies gas to a constantly burning pilot light and a thick pipe supplies liquid gas to the blast valve. When the pilot opens the valve, a powerful jet of flame 9–12 ft (3–4 m) long shoots out, sending a blast of hot air into the envelope. To maintain height, the pilot usually opens the blast valve for a few seconds and then coasts for half a minute.

Thin pipe for propane gas supply to pilot light

Thick pipe for propane liquid supply to blast flame

GAS CYLINDER
The propane gas cylinders are usually made of tough but light aluminum or stainless steel, padded to minimize risk of injury to the passengers in a bumpy landing. Each cylinder holds around 10 gallons (40 liters), enough gas for about 40 minutes' flight.

Blast-flame supply tap drawing liquid from the bottom of the cylinder

Handles for passengers during landing

Suede padding

Pilot-light supply tap drawing gas from the top of the cylinder

THE BASKET
The traditional wicker basket still gives the best combination of lightness and flexible strength. There is no loading ring or hoop on hot air balloons (pp. 8–9). Instead, the basket hangs from the burner frame on stainless-steel cables that loop under the basket and are secured in the weave.

Airship

It seemed that the days of airships were over when they were involved in a number of tragic accidents just before World War II (p. 9), and the giants of the interwar years did indeed vanish. Yet the airship's ability to stay in the air for hour after hour was still useful for tasks such as submarine surveillance. Right up until the late 1960s, small, nonrigid airships filled with safe, nonflammable helium gas were still being made. In the 1980s, a new generation of more substantial airships began to emerge. These ships are made of modern materials, such as carbon-fiber and plastic composites, and filled with helium, not hydrogen, like the early airships.

UP IN FLAMES
Airships filled with hydrogen gas were always in danger from fire. Almost half the 72 airships flown by the German forces in World War I went up in flames, and the inferno that destroyed the *Hindenburg* signaled the end for the giant airships.

Strengthened glass-fiber nose cone to take mooring cable

SKYSHIP 500HL
The first Skyship 500 flew in 1981. It was followed in 1984 by the larger Skyship 600, which is still in service. Although big, at about 170 ft (55 m) long, the Skyship 500 was a fraction of the size of the prewar giant airships, such as the *Hindenburg*, which stretched 800 ft (245 m). In modern airships, such as the Skyships and the Zeppelin NTs (see opposite), it is the pressure of the gas inside that gives them their shape, not a rigid framework as in the prewar giants.

Automatic ballonet valve

Solid ballast for emergencies

Air scoops for filling ballonets

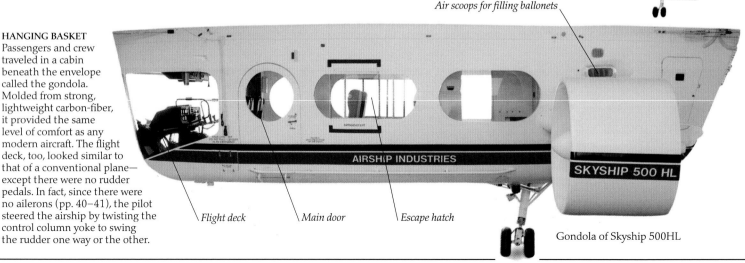

HANGING BASKET
Passengers and crew traveled in a cabin beneath the envelope called the gondola. Molded from strong, lightweight carbon-fiber, it provided the same level of comfort as any modern aircraft. The flight deck, too, looked similar to that of a conventional plane—except there were no rudder pedals. In fact, since there were no ailerons (pp. 40–41), the pilot steered the airship by twisting the control column yoke to swing the rudder one way or the other.

Flight deck

Main door

Escape hatch

AIRSHIP INDUSTRIES

SKYSHIP 500 HL

Gondola of Skyship 500HL

Climbing—rear ballonet is kept fuller and heavier, helping nose to come up

Descending—extra air is blown into front ballonet, bringing nose down

AIR BUBBLES

The Skyship 500's helium-filled envelope contained two air-filled bags called ballonets. As the airship climbed, atmospheric pressure dropped and the gas expanded. Automatic valves opened to release air instead of precious helium (above left). When the airship descended, air was scooped in to refill the ballonets (above right).

RETURN OF THE ZEPPELINS

In 1994, the successor to the original Zeppelin company began developing airships again. The first Zeppelin New Technology (NT) craft flew in 1997. With a crew of two and room for 12 passengers, the NTs are much smaller than the giant Zeppelins of the 1930s, which could carry more than 100 passengers and crew. Nevertheless, the Zeppelin NT is still the biggest airship in the word today.

Rudder to steer the airship left or right

Elevator flaps to help climbing or diving

G-SKSB

Polyester envelope, lined with special gas-proof coating

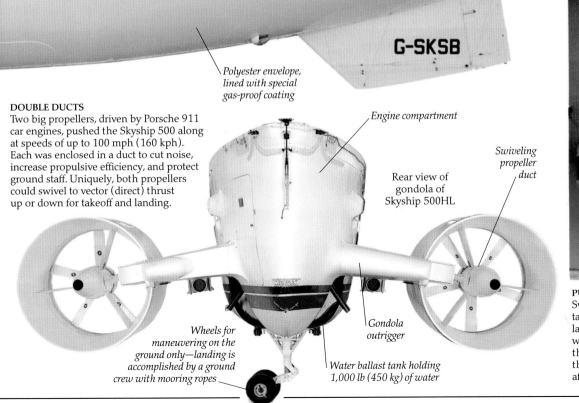

DOUBLE DUCTS

Two big propellers, driven by Porsche 911 car engines, pushed the Skyship 500 along at speeds of up to 100 mph (160 kph). Each was enclosed in a duct to cut noise, increase propulsive efficiency, and protect ground staff. Uniquely, both propellers could swivel to vector (direct) thrust up or down for takeoff and landing.

Engine compartment

Rear view of gondola of Skyship 500HL

Swiveling propeller duct

Wheels for maneuvering on the ground only—landing is accomplished by a ground crew with mooring ropes

Gondola outrigger

Water ballast tank holding 1,000 lb (450 kg) of water

PUSHING UP AND DOWN

Swiveling propellers allow vertical takeoffs. They also help airships to land. Otherwise, precious helium would have to be let out to make the ship heavier—especially when the fuel tank is empty and light after a long flight.

A modern glider

MASTER GLIDER
Birds of prey showed people how to rise up on bubbles of warm air.

Aᴌᴛʜᴏᴜɢʜ ɢʟɪᴅᴇʀs played a prominent part in the pioneering days of aviation (pp. 10–11), interest in them waned after powered flight was achieved. The problem was that, without power, the early gliders could only stay airborne for a few seconds. Then, in the early 1920s, it was found that gliders could ride up on the wind rising over a ridge or hill, so that skilled pilots could stay aloft for hours at a time. A few years later, it was discovered that even away from hills, glider pilots could get a lift from thermals—bubbles of rising air warmed by the ground. Ever since, the sport of gliding has become more and more popular, and the glider has now evolved into one of the most aerodynamically efficient and elegant of all flying machines.

LAUNCHING A GLIDER
Gliders can be launched in various ways. Auto-towing involves using a motor car to pull the glider along on a long cable until it climbs into the air. Winch-launches use a powerful winch in the same way. Both methods are cheap and quick, but will lift the glider no higher than 1,000 ft (300 m) or so. If the pilot cannot find lift from rising air quickly, the flight will last only a few minutes. An aero-tow, using a powered plane to tug the glider into the air (below and right), is much more effective, but time-consuming and expensive.

Tug makes normal takeoff with glider in tow.

Powered tug plane tows glider on a 120-ft (40-m) tow rope.

Airbrakes emerge from the wings at right angles, to steepen the descent for landing

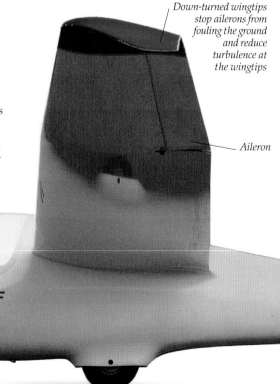

Down-turned wingtips stop ailerons from fouling the ground and reduce turbulence at the wingtips

SLIPPERY SAILPLANE
Modern gliders, such as this Schleicher K23 single-seater, are made from glass-reinforced plastic (GRP). This material is not only strong and light, but can be molded to give a supersmooth, low-drag surface. With such smooth lines and carefully profiled wings, a glider like this is very efficient aerodynamically—with, typically, a glide ratio of better than 1:45. This means it will usually drop only 3 ft (1 m) for every 150 ft (45 m) it flies. Competition gliders perform even better.

Aileron

Instrument panel

BAND AID
In the days when many gliding clubs were on hilltops, a bungee launch was often enough. A team ran toward edge of the hill pulling the glider on an elasticated rope. As the glider "unstuck" from the ground, it catapulted into the air.

Tow rope attached here for winch-launch or auto-tow

Elevator

T-tail

Glider releases tow rope at desired height.

Freed from the glider, the
tug accelerates rapidly and
dives away.

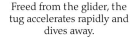

SILENT WINGS
Large gliders like
the Airspeed Horsa
(left) were sometimes
used during World
War II for landing
troops and equipment
silently behind enemy
lines. However, they
were slow and, once
spotted, very vulnerable.

SLIM TUBE
The slim, tapering fuselage is
carefully shaped to minimize drag.
Even around the cockpit, it is as
narrow as possible, and near
the tail it shrinks to a diameter
of less than 1 ft (30 cm).
The tail-fin itself is usually
T-shaped, not only for
aerodynamic performance,
but also to protect the
tailplanes from damage
by tall crops if the glider
has to make a forced
landing in a field.

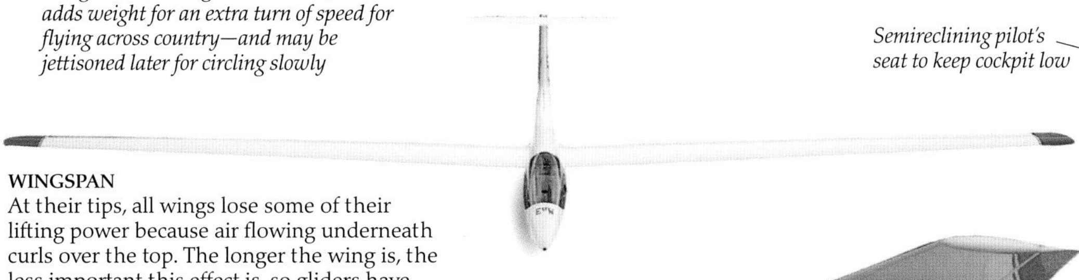

_Wing-tanks holding water ballast, which
adds weight for an extra turn of speed for
flying across country—and may be
jettisoned later for circling slowly_

_Semireclining pilot's
seat to keep cockpit low_

WINGSPAN
At their tips, all wings lose some of their
lifting power because air flowing underneath
curls over the top. The longer the wing is, the
less important this effect is, so gliders have
very long wings.

EVW

Rudder

_Tow rope attached
here for aero-tow_

Kites for people

THE IDEA OF FLYING with a pair of wings alone seemed to have been forgotten after the deaths of Lilienthal (pp. 10–11) and other pioneer gliders around 1900. Then, in the 1940s, an American named Francis Rogallo created a new kite plane using a fabric delta (triangular) wing. It was developed as a steerable parachute for bringing equipment back to Earth from space. But some people began to fly Rogallo wings by hanging beneath the wing and steering it by shifting their body weight. The idea caught on, and hang-gliders were soon running off hills all over the world. Hang-gliding is now one of the world's most popular aerial sports.

SPREADING WINGS
The earliest, Rogallo-type hang-gliders dropped quickly, achieving a glide ratio (p. 58) of only 1:2.5—so flights were exciting, but short. Wings have gradually been improved, however. They are now long and narrow, and more like conventional wings than the original delta shape. A lower fabric skin has also been added to the original single skin to give a more efficient aerofoil section. The result is that glide ratios are now 1:14 or better, and hang-gliders are able, like gliders, to take advantage of thermals and make flights of over 100 miles (160 km).

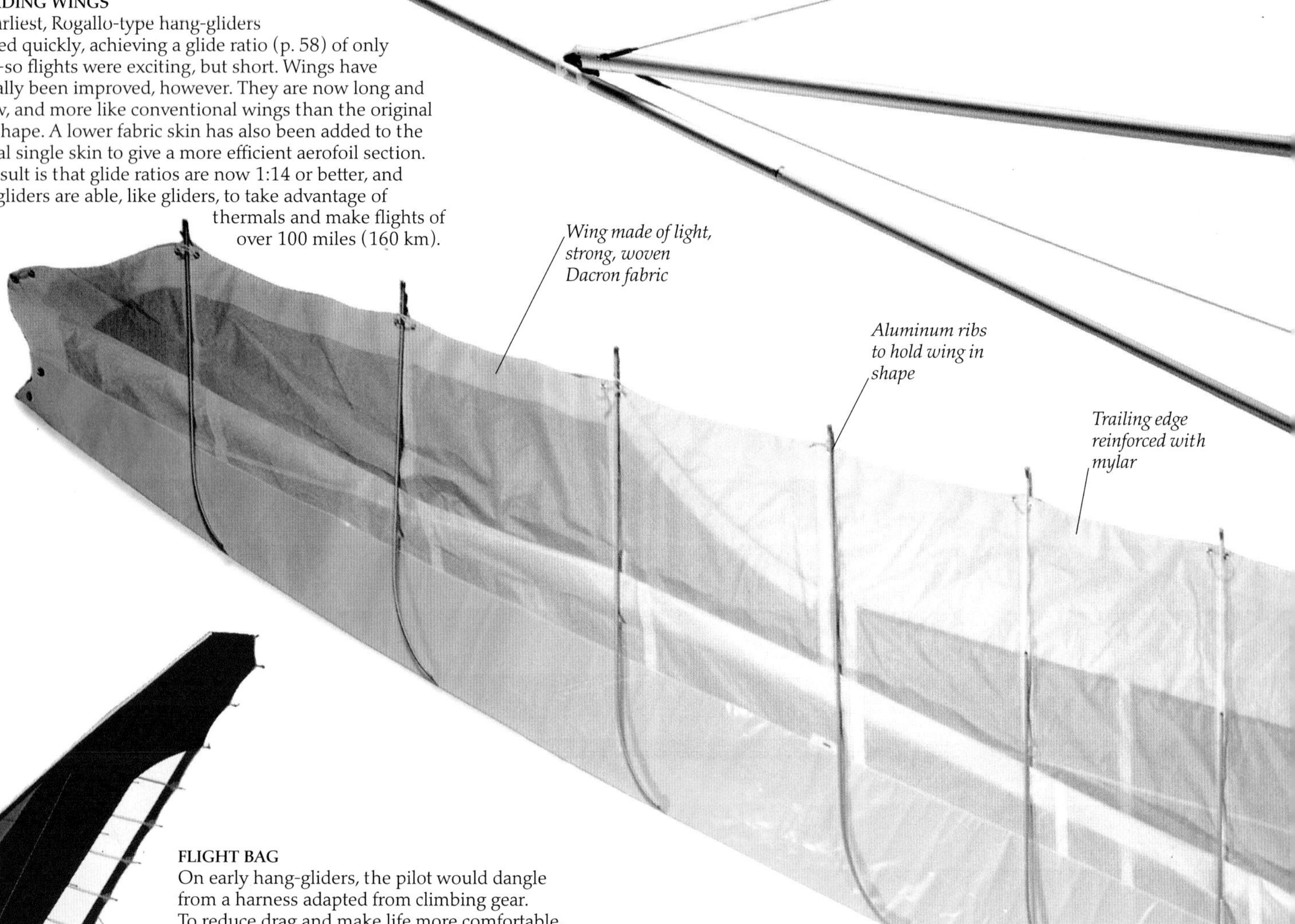

Wing made of light, strong, woven Dacron fabric

Aluminum ribs to hold wing in shape

Trailing edge reinforced with mylar

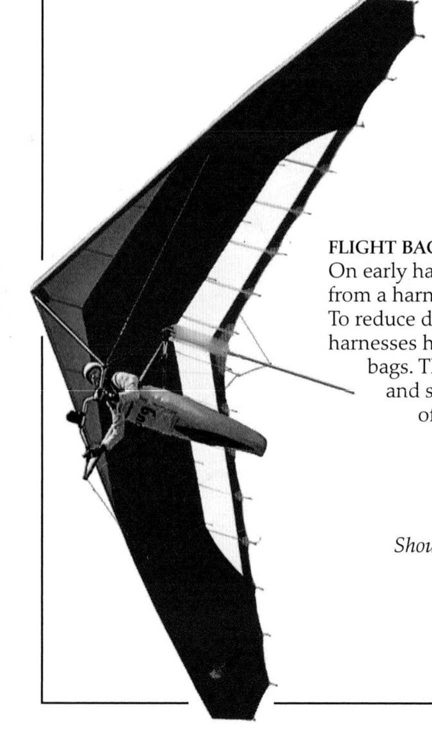

FLIGHT BAG
On early hang-gliders, the pilot would dangle from a harness adapted from climbing gear. To reduce drag and make life more comfortable, harnesses have been replaced by long body bags. These body bags are so supportive and snug that a pilot can make flights of several hours without getting tired or cold.

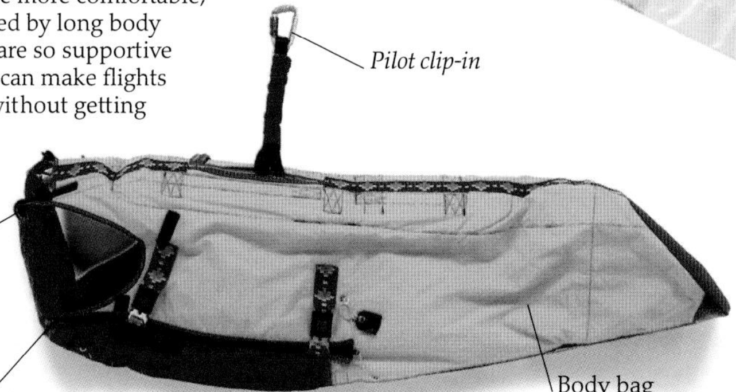

Pilot clip-in

Shoulder strap

Arm-hole

Body bag

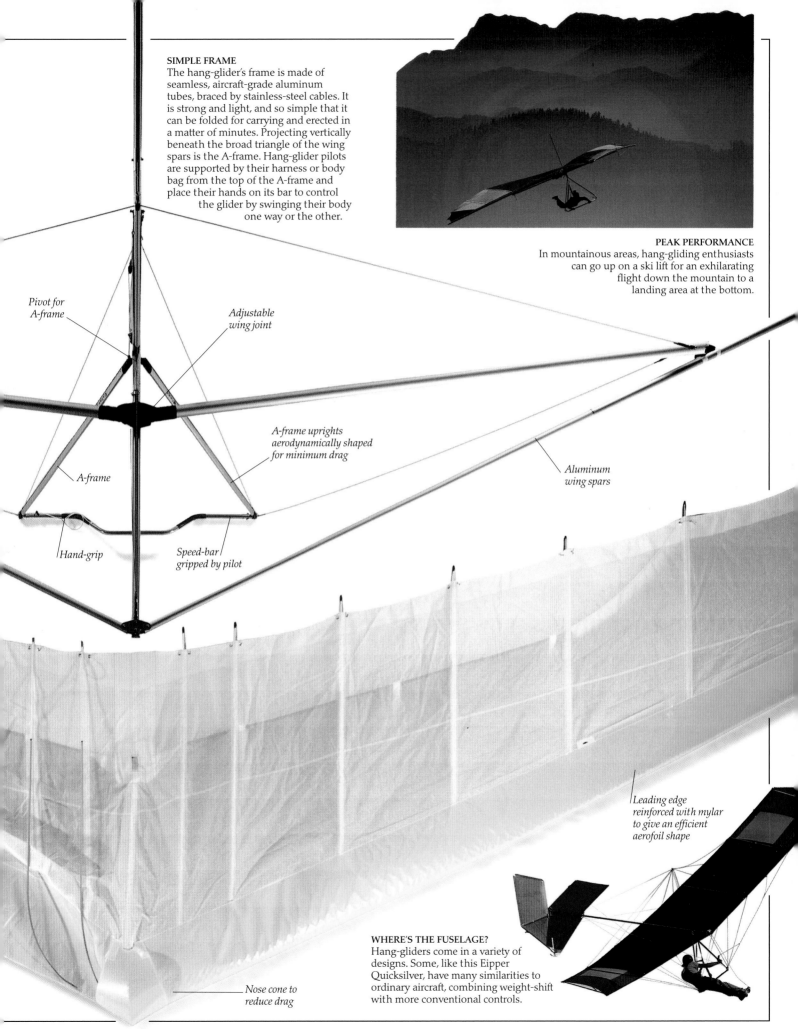

SIMPLE FRAME
The hang-glider's frame is made of seamless, aircraft-grade aluminum tubes, braced by stainless-steel cables. It is strong and light, and so simple that it can be folded for carrying and erected in a matter of minutes. Projecting vertically beneath the broad triangle of the wing spars is the A-frame. Hang-glider pilots are supported by their harness or body bag from the top of the A-frame and place their hands on its bar to control the glider by swinging their body one way or the other.

PEAK PERFORMANCE
In mountainous areas, hang-gliding enthusiasts can go up on a ski lift for an exhilarating flight down the mountain to a landing area at the bottom.

Pivot for A-frame

Adjustable wing joint

A-frame uprights aerodynamically shaped for minimum drag

Aluminum wing spars

A-frame

Hand-grip

Speed-bar gripped by pilot

Leading edge reinforced with mylar to give an efficient aerofoil shape

Nose cone to reduce drag

WHERE'S THE FUSELAGE?
Hang-gliders come in a variety of designs. Some, like this Eipper Quicksilver, have many similarities to ordinary aircraft, combining weight-shift with more conventional controls.

Portable planes

From the first days of powered flying, enthusiasts dreamed of a small aircraft, cheap enough and practical enough to be flown by ordinary people. Yet, until recently, even planes like the basic and popular de Havilland Moth series (p. 43) remained expensive, complicated machines. Then in 1973, Australian hang-glider pioneer Bill Bennett began experimenting with a hang-glider and a chainsaw motor driving a pusher propeller behind the pilot. It was not altogether safe, but it worked, and the ultralight was born. Since then, the way the engine is fitted has become much more practical and safe, and the frame has been improved to take the extra load. Ultralights (or microlights, as they are sometimes known) are flown all over the world. Some retain flexible wings (flex-wing) like hang-gliders. Others, especially in the US and Australia, have developed into miniature aircraft with fixed wings and control surfaces.

Aluminum wing spar

Tensioning cable

THE FIRST ULTRALIGHT?
Brazilian pioneer Alberto Santos-Dumont's tiny No. 19 monoplane had a wingspan of just 18 ft (6 m) and was perhaps the first ultralight. He designed it in Paris in 1907 as an aerial "runaround," and could de-rig it to carry it on his car.

WIDE WING
Like the hang-glider on pages 60–61, a flex-wing ultralight like this Solar Wings Pegasus Q has a shallow triangular wing made of Dacron. But it is broader than the hang-glider in order to lift the extra weight of the engine, trike, and two crew members.

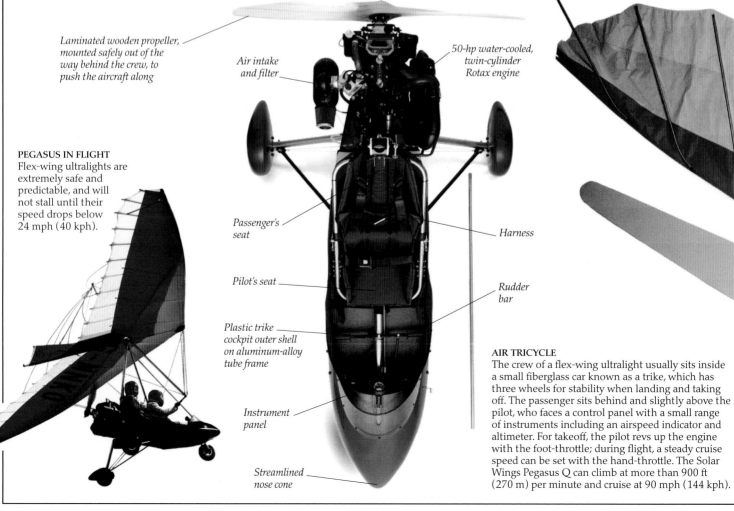

Laminated wooden propeller, mounted safely out of the way behind the crew, to push the aircraft along

Air intake and filter

50-hp water-cooled, twin-cylinder Rotax engine

PEGASUS IN FLIGHT
Flex-wing ultralights are extremely safe and predictable, and will not stall until their speed drops below 24 mph (40 kph).

Passenger's seat

Harness

Pilot's seat

Rudder bar

Plastic trike cockpit outer shell on aluminum-alloy tube frame

Instrument panel

Streamlined nose cone

AIR TRICYCLE
The crew of a flex-wing ultralight usually sits inside a small fiberglass car known as a trike, which has three wheels for stability when landing and taking off. The passenger sits behind and slightly above the pilot, who faces a control panel with a small range of instruments including an airspeed indicator and altimeter. For takeoff, the pilot revs up the engine with the foot-throttle; during flight, a steady cruise speed can be set with the hand-throttle. The Solar Wings Pegasus Q can climb at more than 900 ft (270 m) per minute and cruise at 90 mph (144 kph).

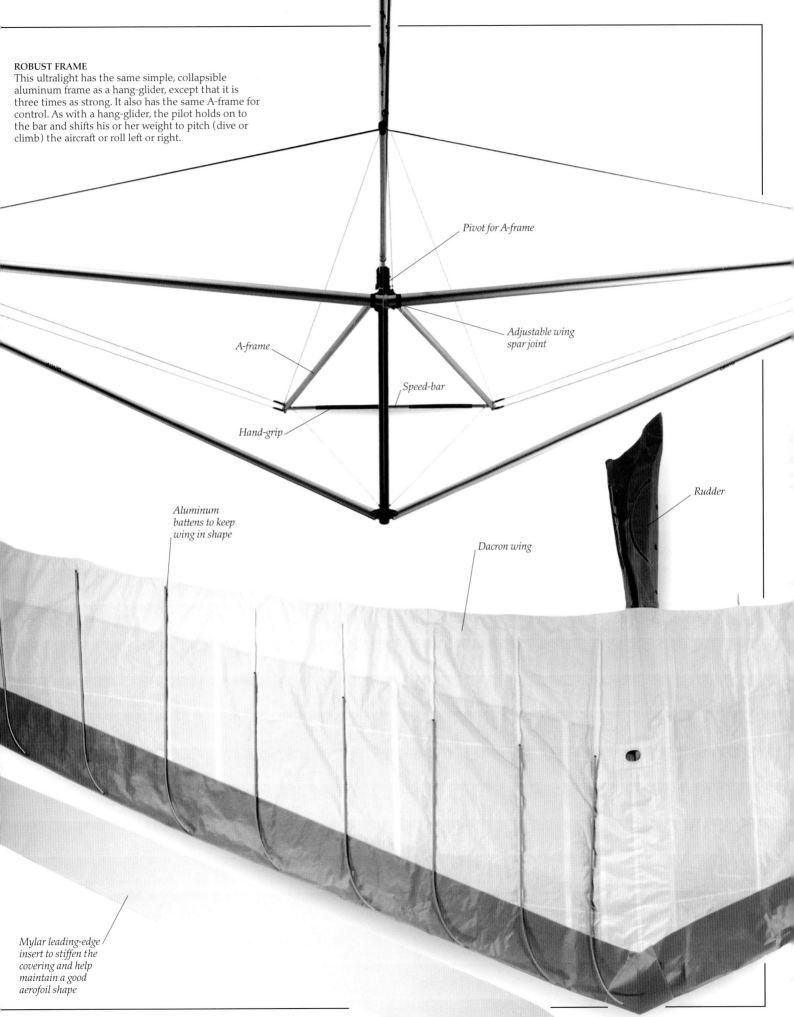

ROBUST FRAME
This ultralight has the same simple, collapsible
aluminum frame as a hang-glider, except that it is
three times as strong. It also has the same A-frame for
control. As with a hang-glider, the pilot holds on to
the bar and shifts his or her weight to pitch (dive or
climb) the aircraft or roll left or right.

Pivot for A-frame

*Adjustable wing
spar joint*

A-frame

Speed-bar

Hand-grip

Rudder

*Aluminum
battens to keep
wing in shape*

Dacron wing

*Mylar leading-edge
insert to stiffen the
covering and help
maintain a good
aerofoil shape*

63

Did you know?

AMAZING FACTS

Wright brothers' first flight

The first passengers in a free flight were a sheep, a duck, and a rooster, which in 1783 flew in a wicker basket suspended from a balloon designed by the Montgolfier brothers.

The first aerial stowaway was a young Frenchman named Fontaine, who jumped into a Montgolfier hot-air balloon just as it was taking off in January 1784.

The *Flyer* made four flights on December 17, 1903, with the Wright brothers taking turns flying. The longest flight of the day (59 seconds) was made by Wilbur, at 853 ft (260 m).

The first woman to make a solo flight was Baroness Raymonde de Laroche, in 1909. A year later, she became the first woman to receive a pilot's license, granted by the Aéro Club of France.

The first solo flight across the Atlantic was made by Charles Lindbergh in 1927, in a Ryan monoplane called the *Spirit of St. Louis*. One of his challenges on the 33.5-hour flight was to stay awake. He did this by pinching himself and opening the aircraft's side window to get blasts of fresh air.

The first helicopter flight was made by French mechanic Paul Cornu in 1907, when his machine lifted and hovered for 20 seconds.

The Blue Max (the nickname of the Ordre pour le Merite, the highest German honor for service in World War I) was named after flying ace Max Immelmann.

In the early days of flying, one of the most famous awards was the Schneider Trophy. The first Schneider seaplane air race, held in Monaco in 1913, was won by Maurice Prevost, the only pilot to complete the course. His plane traveled at an average speed of 45.7 mph (73.6 kph).

In 1929, the first all-woman air race took place in the United States, from Santa Monica, California, to Cleveland, Ohio. The contestants included Amelia Earhart (p. 67).

The Boeing 747-400ER can fly about 8,800 miles (14,200 km) without stopping to refuel.

The longest muscle-powered flight was made by Greek cycle champion Kanellos Kanellopoulos in the *Daedalus* in 1988, pedaling nearly 75 miles (120 km) in 4 hours.

Schneider Trophy poster

In 1999, the *Breitling Orbiter 3* piloted by Bertrand Piccard and Brian Jones, became the first balloon to fly nonstop around the world. In 2002, American Steve Fossett did this solo, making a 13-day flight.

In 2006, Steve Fossett made the fastest solo around-the-world plane flight. He circled the globe in 67 hours and 2 minutes in the specially built Virgin Atlantic *GlobalFlyer*. In 2010, Swiss aviator Riccardo Mortara and his two-man crew completed the fastest team flight around the world. They circumnavigated the globe in a Rockwell Sabreliner 65 jet, taking 57 hours and 54 minutes.

Charles Lindbergh

Steve Fossett

QUESTIONS AND ANSWERS

Q Who was the first person in history to fly?

A The first person to fly in free flight was Jean-François Pilâtre de Rozier, who, accompanied by the Marquis d'Arlandes, flew for 23 minutes and traveled 5.5 miles (9 km) in a Montgolfier balloon on November 21, 1783. However, the world's first aviator is considered to be Otto Lilienthal, who invented a practical hang-glider and became the first person to make repeated controlled flights in the early 1890s. Orville Wright made the world's first powered airplane flight on December 17, 1903, at Kitty Hawk, North Carolina, in the *Flyer*. The flight lasted a mere 12 seconds, and the aircraft traveled just 120 ft (37 m).

Airbus A380

Q What is the world's largest commercial plane?

A The Airbus A380 made its maiden flight in 2005, and entered service in 2007 with Singapore Airlines. It has a wingspan of almost 262 ft (80 m) and floor space of about 3,450 sq ft (320 sq m)—49 percent more than the next largest airliner, the Boeing 747-400. The A380 can seat 525 people in a typical three-class configuration, or up to 853 people in all-economy class configurations.

Q How did the first aviators manage to find their way?

A The first airplanes had no instruments, so to find out where they were, aviators simply looked out of the plane for landmarks, such as a church tower or railroad line. To find their height, they had small pocket altimeters similar to those used by mountaineers.

Q Why are the blades of an aircraft propeller twisted?

A A propeller blade spins faster at the tips than at the center. Twisting the blade ensures that uniform thrust is produced along its entire length, even though different parts of it are spinning at different speeds.

Q Why was the Concorde banned?

A Despite being the fastest airliner ever, the Concorde was banned from some airports because its turbojets were very noisy during takeoff and landing. It was also prevented from flying at supersonic speeds over land because of the loud "supersonic boom" it made as it crossed the sound barrier.

Q What does the future look like for airships?

A Today, airships are used mainly for pleasure flights and advertising, but in the future they may find roles in defense and security. The US Army is investigating the possibility of developing huge, unmanned reconnaissance airships that would float high over war zones gathering data, staying airborne for weeks at a time. These craft will actually be "hybrid" airships, meaning that they will use a combination of thrusters and lighter-than-air gas to remain aloft.

German LVG CVI, 1917 — *Twisted propeller*

Record breakers

LARGEST AIRPLANE
The Hughes H-4 Hercules flying boat, the *Spruce Goose*, was the world's largest airplane, with a wingspan measuring 320 ft (97.5 m).

SMALLEST AIRPLANE
The smallest biplane is *Bumble Bee Two*, which is just 8.7 ft (2.64 m) long and weighs 400 lb (180 kg).

HEAVIEST AIRPLANE
The Antonov An-225 *Mriya* (meaning "Dream") is the heaviest aircraft ever to fly, weighing a staggering 660 tons (600 metric tons). The plane has six engines, and its cargo hold is 142 ft (43 m) long.

FASTEST COMMERCIAL AIRLINER
The Concorde, which was retired from service in 2003, had a maximum cruising speed of Mach 2.05, or 1,354 mph (2,179 kph)—twice the speed of sound. Although it could travel over twice as fast as the Boeing 747, it could seat just 128 passengers.

BUSIEST AIRPORT
Hartsfield International Airport in Atlanta, Georgia, was the world's busiest airport in 2008, both in terms of takeoffs and landings (more than 970,000) and passenger numbers (around 88 millon).

Hartsfield International Airport, Atlanta, Georgia

Proposed Northrop-Grumman Long-Endurance Multi-Intelligence Vehicle

Who's who?

THE HUGE ADVANCES IN AVIATION made in the last 100 years were only possible because of the bravery and dedication of the pioneers of early flying machines. Here are some of those pioneers, and a few of the many people involved in the production of great aircraft, from designers and engineers to manufacturers and test pilots.

PIONEERS OF FLIGHT

JOSEPH AND ÉTIENNE MONTGOLFIER
French inventors Joseph (1740–1810) and Étienne (1745–1799) were sons of a paper manufacturer from southeast France. Interested in how paper was lifted up a chimney when put on a fire, they created the first hot-air balloon in 1782.

GEORGE CAYLEY (1773–1857)
English engineer and pioneer of aviation who developed the basic principles of heavier-than-air flight. Cayley was the first inventor to figure out how a wing works, and to realize the advantages of having a cambered wing surface. In 1853, Cayley built the first successful person-carrying glider.

HENRI GIFFARD (1825–1882)
French engineer and inventor who, in 1852, built a cigar-shaped balloon equipped with a rudder, propeller, and light steam engine. He succeeded in steering it for 17 miles (27 km). Giffard's balloon was the forerunner of the modern dirigible, or airship.

Otto Lilienthal

FERDINAND VON ZEPPELIN (1838–1917)
German army officer who constructed a dirigible or rigid airship, named a Zeppelin, between 1897 and 1900, which first flew on July 2, 1900. Zeppelin later set up a company to build a fleet of airships.

CLÉMENT ADER (1841–1925)
French engineer who built a steam-powered, bat-winged plane called *Éole* between 1882 and 1890, making the first piloted powered takeoff in it in October 1890 and traveling a distance of 165 ft (50 m).

OTTO LILIENTHAL (1848–1896)
German aeronautical inventor and pioneer of gliders who studied the flight of birds in order to build a heavier-than-air flying machine. He published a book based on his research called *Bird Flight as the Basis of Aviation* (1889). Lilienthal then built a series of fixed-wing monoplane and biplane gliders, making over 2,000 flights. He was killed in a flying accident near Berlin when the wind blew his glider out of control.

Wilbur Wright and the *Flyer*

ORVILLE AND WILBUR WRIGHT
The brothers Orville (1871–1948) and Wilbur (1867–1912) were self-taught American airplane pioneers and the first to fly in a heavier-than-air powered aircraft, the *Flyer*, at Kitty Hawk, North Carolina, on December 17, 1903. They patented their flying machine and, in 1909, formed an aircraft production company.

LOUIS BLÉRIOT (1872–1936)
French airman who pioneered the monoplane aircraft with a single wing, separate tail, and front engine. On July 25, 1909, he made the first flight across the English Channel in his small Type XI aircraft, becoming an instant celebrity.

INVENTORS, ENGINEERS, AND DESIGNERS

ELMER AMBROSE SPERRY (1860–1930)
American inventor of the gyro compass and, for airplanes, the directional gyro, the gyro horizon, and the drift indicator. His son, Lawrence Sperry (1892–1923), designed a retractable undercarriage.

IGOR IVANOVICH SIKORSKY (1889–1972)
Russian-born aeronautical engineer who built airplanes, flying boats, and, in 1939, the first successful helicopter, the VS-300.

SIDNEY CAMM (1893–1966)
English aircraft designer at Hawker Siddeley Aviation whose designs included the Fury, Hart, and Demon biplanes; the jet-engined Sea Hawk; and the Harrier Jump-Jet.

Igor Ivanovich Sikorsky

JUAN DE LA CIERVA (1895–1936)
Spanish inventor of the autogiro—a rotor craft with a freely rotating wing—that aimed to be a safe form of air transportation.

FRANK WHITTLE (1907–1996)
British pioneer of jet aircraft who trained as a pilot in the RAF (Royal Air Force), becoming a test pilot. He devised a jet-propelling, gas-turbine engine, later used in a Gloster aircraft in 1941. His invention led to the worldwide use of jets in high-speed, high-flying aircraft.

HANS VON OHAIN (1911–1998)
German-American engineer who invented a jet engine independently of Frank Whittle. Ohain's engine powered the world's first jet aircraft, the prototype Heinkel He-178, but the plane never went into full production.

MANUFACTURERS

William Edward Boeing

GEOFFREY DE HAVILLAND (1882–1965)
British aircraft designer and test pilot. He started his own company in 1920, building the DH-60 Moth light airplane, the Mosquito, and the Comet, the first jetliner.

ERNST HEINRICH HEINKEL (1888–1958)
German aircraft engineer who, in 1922, began making seaplanes, flying boats, and military aircraft. He also built the first jet plane, the He-178, in 1939 and the first rocket-powered aircraft, the He-176.

ALLAN HAINES LOCKHEED (1889–1969)
American aircraft manufacturer who started the Alco Hydro-Airplane Company in 1913, then, in 1916, Loughhead Aircraft, which was relaunched as the Lockheed Aircraft Company in 1926.

ANTHONY FOKKER (1890–1939)
Dutch aircraft engineer who founded the Fokker aircraft factory in Germany in 1913, which made aircraft for the German air force during World War I. He emigrated to the US in 1922, becoming president of the Fokker Aircraft Corporation of America.

DONALD WILLS DOUGLAS (1892–1981)
American designer and manufacturer of aircraft who set up a company called David-Douglas Co. in 1920. The company's successful aircraft included the Douglas World Cruisers— two of which made an historic around-the-world flight in 1924—and the jet-engined DC-3, DC-8, DC-9, and DC-10. The company merged with the McDonnell Aircraft Corporation in 1967, to become McDonnell Douglas.

Donald Wills Douglas

HUGO JUNKERS (1859–1935)
German aircraft engineer whose company built the first successful all-metal plane in 1915, and the first light-alloy plane in 1916.

WILLIAM EDWARD BOEING (1881–1956)
American aircraft manufacturer who formed the Pacific Aero Products Company in 1916. The company was renamed the Boeing Airplane Company in 1917, becoming the world's largest maker of aircraft. In 1997, Boeing merged with McDonnell Douglas to become The Boeing Company.

AVIATORS

Amelia Earhart

CHARLES KINGSFORD SMITH (1897–1935)
Australian pilot who made the first flight across the Pacific from the US to Australia, in 1928. In the same year, Smith made the first nonstop flight across Australia and the first flight from Australia to New Zealand. He also formed Australian National Airways. Kingsford Smith and his crew later disappeared over the Bay of Bengal.

AMELIA EARHART (1897–1937)
American aviator and the first woman to fly the Atlantic, from Newfoundland to Wales, on June 17, 1928, in a Lockheed Vega. Earhart and her navigator, Fred Noonan, disappeared over the Pacific in July 1937 during an attempt to fly around the world.

WILEY POST (1899–1935)
American aviator who set a record time for flying around the world in the Lockheed Vega *Winnie Mae* in June 1931, with navigator Harold Gatty. The trip took 8 days, 15 hours, and 51 minutes. Two years later, Post became the first person to fly solo around the world. Wiley Post was killed in an air crash in 1935.

CHARLES AUGUSTUS LINDBERGH (1902–1974)
American aviator who worked as an airmail pilot and became famous after he made the first solo nonstop flight across the Atlantic, from New York to Paris, in May 1927 in his plane the *Spirit of St. Louis*.

AMY JOHNSON (1903–1941)
British aviator who got her pilot's license in 1928 and, just two years later, made a solo flight from England to Australia in 19.5 days. Johnson made the trip in a de Havilland DH-60 Moth nicknamed "Jason."

CHARLES "CHUCK" YEAGER (1923–)
American test pilot who fought with the US Army Air Corps during World War II. Yeager became the first person to fly faster than the speed of sound, at around 700 mph (1,100 kph), or Mach 1.06, on October 14, 1947, in a Bell XS-1 rocket plane. The plane was nicknamed "Glennis," after Yeager's wife.

ARTHUR WHITTEN BROWN (1886–1948)
British aviator and navigator with John William Alcock on the first nonstop crossing of the Atlantic.

MAX IMMELMANN (1890–1916)
Flying ace of World War I. He had an aerial maneuver (the Immelmann turn) named after him, comprising of a half-loop then a half-roll. It was said to be a way for pilots to escape pursuit or mount an attack. Max Immelmann was killed in action in 1916.

JOHN WILLIAM ALCOCK (1892–1919)
English aviator who, in June 1919, with Arthur Whitten Brown as navigator, became the first to fly across the Atlantic nonstop from Newfoundland to Ireland. Shortly afterward, Alcock was killed in an airplane accident in France.

Charles "Chuck" Yeager

Find out more

YOU CAN FIND OUT about the history of air travel by visiting museums, where you can see some of the famous early planes of the pioneers, or even try out a flight simulator. There are also airshows and ballooning events around the world where it is possible to see all kinds of civil and military aircraft, hot-air balloons, and airships up close. The internet is a great resource for finding out about events that you cannot attend in person.

TAKE A RIDE
At some museums and air shows, it is possible to take to the sky in an airplane. For example, visitors to the Old Rhinebeck Aerodrome in New York State, can have a ride in an open-cockpit biplane (pictured above). You can also go up in a vintage Tiger Moth or de Havilland Dragon Rapide at the UK's Imperial War Museum in Duxford, Cambridgeshire.

2009 Dutch Balloon Trophy, Wezuperbrug, Netherlands

BALLOONING EVENTS
Many countries have their own national balloon championships and local festivals at which you can see the latest models of competitive and fiesta balloons. The World Ballooning Championships are held every two years. The 19th Championships were held at Debrecen, Hungary, in 2010.

Features include long, thin wings, a U-shaped tail, and engines partly embedded in the fuselage

Airbus Concept Plane

IN THE PRESS
New developments in aviation are often reported in the media. For example, the Airbus Concept Plane—the Airbus company's vision of how airliners could look by the mid-21st century—was revealed to the press during the 2010 Farnborough International airshow in the UK.

AIRSHOWS
Many countries hold airshows at which you can see exhibits from all over the world. The Paris Airshow began in 1908 and is currently held at Le Bourget Airport in Paris, France. The UK's Farnborough International, an airshow organized by the Society of British Aerospace Companies, occurs every two years just west of London. The 2010 show, which had more than 150 aircraft either flying or on static display and hundreds more exhibits, attracted nearly 230,000 visitors. The annual London Airshow and Balloon Festival, held at London International Airport in Ontario, Canada, allows visitors to get up close to aircraft, watch flying displays, and even take balloon and helicopter rides.

Aircraft and crowds at the 2009 Fairford Airshow, Gloucestershire, UK

One of the Red Arrows' 12 Hawk jet trainer aircraft

AERIAL DISPLAYS

At many airshows and other events, you can see daring aeronautical displays. One of the most famous aeronautical teams is the Royal Air Force's Red Arrows. If you cannot see them in person, you can find news, photos, and details of their maneuvers at www.raf.mod.uk/reds.

When pod closes, screen shows film of flight, as seen through the cockpit of a Red Arrows jet

HANDS-ON

Some museums, such the Science Museum in London, UK, have hands-on displays where you can try out an aircraft flight simulator with feed-in and feed-back computer data. The Science Museum also has a 3-D motion effects exhibit that gives you an idea of what it is like to fly with the Red Arrows aerobatic team. Some computer game companies make flight simulation games that allow you to test your flying and landing skills in all kinds of weather conditions.

Fly 3-D exhibit, Science Museum, London, UK

Plane watchers gather near Heathrow Airport, London, to see the first visit of the Airbus A380 to the UK in 2006

PLANE WATCHING

Some airports, especially smaller ones, have spectator galleries where visitors can see planes land, refuel, and take off. Even if such facilities do not exist, there may be areas beside the runways where you are allowed to watch the planes come and go. At some busy airports, as many as 50 aircraft take off and land every hour. Some people go especially to spot particular types of aircraft, looking for the distinctive insignia and colors of different national airlines.

USEFUL WEBSITES

- Interactive information on airplanes, piloting, and design: **kids.msfc.nasa.gov/Rockets/Airplanes/**
- Information about upcoming air show events in the United States and Canada: **www.airshows.com/**
- News about Boeing and its planes: **www.boeing.com**
- Details on the aviation history of North America and state-by-state listings of air museums: **www.aerofiles.com**
- Details about the Sun-N-Fun Celebration flight: **www.sun-n-fun.org**

Museums to visit

SMITHSONIAN INSTITUTION NATIONAL AIR AND SPACE MUSEUM, WASHINGTON, D.C.
www.nasm.si.edu/
This huge museum has more than 350 aircraft in its collection, many of which are on display. Worth seeing are the historic Wright 1903 *Flyer*, the Ryan *Spirit of St. Louis*, and the Bell X-1.

THE NEW ENGLAND AIR MUSEUM, WINDSOR LOCKS, CT
www.neam.org
This aviation museum holds many fascinating exhibits, from aircraft and engine displays to the Tuskegee Airmen, Early French Aviation, and a History of Air Mall.

THE INTREPID SEA, AIR, AND SPACE MUSEUM, NEW YORK, NY
www.intrepidmuseum.org
The scale of this old aircraft carrier gives the Intrepid museum an impressive backdrop to its aircraft collection, including the A-6 Intruder and the FJ-3 Fury, which once actually flew off the Intrepid as part of her air group.

SAN DIEGO AEROSPACE MUSEUM, SAN DIEGO, CA
www.aerospacemuseum.org/links.html
Air travel unfolds at the large San Diego Aerospace Museum with a model of the Montgolfier brothers hot-air balloon of 1783 and follows with exhibits charting the dawn of powered flight, air combat in World War 1, and beyond. Highlights include a Spitfire MK OV-1, an A-4 Skyhawk jet, and a Navy F6F Hellcat.

EEA AIRVENTURE MUSEUM, OSHKOSH, WI
http://museum.eea.org/
The museum hosts the largest air show in the US. This large museum houses a collection of more than 250 historic airplanes and boasts five movie theaters. The "hands-on" Hanger X is an exciting interactive gallery for kids of all ages. Also not to be missed is the Eagle Hanger, which displays a tribute to World War II aviation.

NATIONAL MUSEUM OF THE UNITED STATES AIR FORCE, DAYTON, OH
www.nationalmuseum.af.mil
The National Museum of the United States Air Force is the largest and oldest military aviation museum in the world. This unique free attraction tells the exciting story of aviation development from the days of the Wright Brothers at Kitty Hawk to the present. Each year over one million visitors tour 10 acres of indoor exhibits, featuring over 400 aircraft and missiles and thousands of artifacts including personal memorabilia, uniforms, and photographs.

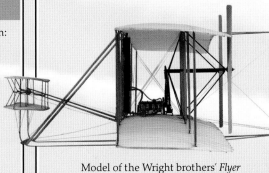

Model of the Wright brothers' *Flyer*

Glossary

Airship: ABC Lightship A-60+, 1994

AERODYNAMICS The study of the movement of objects through air.

AEROFOIL Curved wing shape in which the upper surface is longer (from leading to trailing edge) than the lower surface.

AILERON Flap on an airplane's trailing edge enabling an airplane to tilt to one side (rolling or banking).

AIRBRAKE Surface that can be extended from an aircraft's wings to slow it down or steepen its descent.

AIRSHIP Long, thin, lighter-than-air craft usually filled with helium or hot air; often steered by swiveling propellers to help with takeoff and landing.

ALTIMETER Instrument used to measure an airplane's altitude, or height off the ground.

ARTIFICIAL HORIZON Instrument used to indicate an aircraft's position in relation to the horizon, enabling a pilot to land more safely in poor weather or at night; often called a gyro-horizon.

AUTOGIRO Craft with a conventional propeller and also a rotor that is spun by the action of air flowing through its disk from below; forerunner of the helicopter.

AUTOMATIC PILOT Also called an autopilot, an electronic system that automatically stabilizes an aircraft and can put it back on its original flight path after a disturbance, such as turbulence. In modern aircraft, the autopilot can be set so that the aircraft follows a certain course.

BALLONET Air-filled compartment inside an airship's envelope (which contains lighter-than-air helium gas). It is used to control the airship's height. Letting air out of the ballonet makes the airship lighter, so it rises; pumping air in makes the airship heavier, so it sinks.

BIPLANE Fixed-wing aircraft with two wings.

BOGIE Type of landing leg on an aircraft with two or more pairs of wheels.

CAMBER Curve on the wing section of an airplane.

COCKPIT Compartment in an airplane's fuselage for the pilot(s) and, sometimes, other crew.

DIRIGIBLE Able to be steered; another name for an airship.

DOPE Airplane varnish painted onto fabric to make it stronger and tighter.

DRAG Pressure of air slowing down an airplane when in flight.

DRIFT INDICATOR Instrument that shows an airplane's angle of drift (its sideways movement because of crosswind).

ELEVATOR Flap on a plane's tail that enables the plane to move up or down (called pitching).

ELEVONS Control surfaces on wings, with the same functions as ailerons and elevators.

Eurocopter HH-65 Dolphin helicopter, 1994

ENVELOPE Casing (usually coated in nylon) of an airship that contains the gas used to provide lift.

FLYING BOAT Airplane with a watertight hull, which allows it to move on water.

FUSELAGE Body of an aircraft; from the French word *fuseler*, meaning "to shape like a spindle."

GLASS COCKPIT Cockpit in which traditional instruments such as dials are replaced by electronic displays on glass screens or, more usually, liquid-crystal displays (LCDs).

GLIDE RATIO How far forward an aircraft travels for every meter it descends when it is gliding unpowered. A glide ratio of 1:45 means that the aircraft drops by 1 m (3 ft) for every 45 m (150 ft) it flies.

GLIDER Unpowered aircraft with a wide wingspan that uses currents of hot, rising air (thermals) to stay airborne; controlled with a rudder, elevators, and ailerons.

GONDALA The cabin of an airship, in which the passengers and crew travel.

HANG-GLIDER Unpowered craft that uses thermals for lift, made of material stretched across a simple frame to form a wing. The pilot hangs below the wing in a harness or body bag, and steers by shifting his or her weight from side to side.

HELICOPTER Aircraft powered, lifted, and steered by rotating blades. A helicopter can take off vertically, fly slowly, hover, and move in any direction. Helicopters are often used for traffic surveillance and rescue work because of their maneuverability.

HOT-AIR BALLOON Lighter-than-air craft used mainly for recreation. Modern hot-air balloons use propane burners carried above the balloon's basket to heat up the air inside the envelope (*see also* ENVELOPE).

Hughes H-4 Hercules flying boat, the *Spruce Goose*, 1947

JOYSTICK Control column used to steer an aircraft so it can dive, climb, or roll.

LEADING EDGE The front edge of (for example) a wing, rotor, or tail.

LIFT Upward force created by the way in which air flows around an aircraft wing (*see also* AEROFOIL).

LONGERON Part of an aircraft's structure that runs the length of the fuselage.

MACH NUMBER Ratio of an airplane's air speed to the velocity of sound, or speed of sound, in the given conditions (such as height, air density, and temperature); named after the Austrian physicist Ernst Mach (1838–1916). Mach 1 is the speed of sound, or about 659 mph (1,060 kph) at 36,000 ft (11,000 m); Mach 2 is twice the speed of sound, and so on.

MONOCOQUE Fuselage with no internal bracing, in which nearly all the structural load is carried by the skin.

MONOPLANE Fixed-single-wing aircraft.

Solar Wings Pegasus Microlight, 1989

NONRIGID Type of airship with no internal framework, in which shape is maintained by the pressure of gas and air ballonets inside.

ORNITHOPTER Aircraft propelled by flapping wings.

PITCH Rotating or tilting of a aircraft nose-up and nose-down by raising or lowering the elevators on the tailplane (*see also* ELEVATOR, TAILPLANE).

PROPELLER Rotating blades that drive an aircraft forward.

RIGID Airship with an internal framework.

ROLL Movement of an aircraft in which one wing tip rises and the other falls; roll is controlled by adjusting the ailerons.

RUDDER Vertical, flat surface for steering an airplane to the right or left.

SCARFF RING Mounting for hand-operated machine-guns used in British airplanes from 1916 until the 1930s. It allowed gunners to swivel the gun and fire in many directions.

SPAR Structural support in a wing running the length of the wing.

SPEED OF SOUND The speed of sound is around 761 mph (1,225 kph) at sea level, but falls the higher you go into the sky. Above an altitude of around 3,280 ft (1,000 m) the speed of sound stays the same, at about 659 mph (1,060 kph).

STALL When aircraft's lift is lost, causing the plane to pitch downward and possibly go into a spin.

STRUT Vertical support or brace that resists pressure; for example, between the longerons in a fuselage (*see also* FUSELAGE, LONGERON).

SUPERCHARGER Device that forces extra air into an airplane's engine to increase power at high altitudes.

SUPERSONIC Faster than the speed of sound.

TAILPLANE Wings at the back of an aircraft to provide stability when pitching and to which the elevators are often attached (*see also* PITCH).

TILT-ROTOR Aircraft with rotors that enable it to take off vertically, swivel, then be powered forward.

TRAILING EDGE The rear edge of (for example) a wing, rotor, or tail.

TRIPLANE Fixed-wing aircraft with three wings, such as the German Fokker Triplane of the early 1900s.

TURBOFAN Type of gas-turbine engine in which some of the power drives a fan that pushes out air with the exhaust, thereby increasing thrust. Turbofans are used in most airliners because they are more economical and less noisy than turbojet engines.

Avro Triplane IV, 1910

TURBOJET Simple type of gas turbine (jet) engine in which a compressor forces air into a combustion chamber, where fuel is burned, and the hot gases produced spin a turbine that drives the compressor. Turbojets are noisier than the turbofans used by most airliners. The Concorde was powered by turbojets.

TURBOPROP Type of gas turbine engine connected to a propeller and used to power it (*see also* PROPELLER).

ULTRALIGHT Powered hang-glider with a small engine and an open fiberglass car called a trike. Ultralights are sometimes known as microlights.

UNDERCARRIAGE Another name for an airplane's landing gear.

VECTORED THRUST Way of moving an aircraft by swiveling its propellers or the tail pipe of its jet engine so that the thrust pushes the aircraft in another direction. Some airships and fighter planes use vectored thrust.

WIDE-BODIED Name given to commercial airplanes with wide internal cabins, allowing for three sets of seating in each row and two aisles between the sets.

WING-WARPING Way of controlling an airplane's ability to bank or roll by torsion (twisting) of the outer wing edges instead of using ailerons.

YAW Turning movement to one side or the other made by adjusting an aircraft's rudder.

Interior of a Boeing 747, a wide-bodied aircraft, 1989

Index

AB

Ader, Clément 13, 66
Aerial Steam Carriage 12–13
aerobatics 16, 22, 41, 42
Aerodrome 13
aerofoil 30, 31
aileron 23, 26, 27, 33, 34, 35, 41, 58, 70
airbrake 34, 58, 70
Airbus A320 44–45
  A320 44–45
  A380 65
airframe 15, 19, 20, 21, 23–25, 32, 34
airliner 20, 32–33, 34–35, 36, 39, 44–45
airport 65
airship 9, 56–57, 65, 70
airshows 68
airspeed 32, 43, 45, 46–47
Airspeed Horsa 59
Alcock, John 32, 42, 67
Allison engine 51
altimeter 42, 43, 44, 46–47, 65, 70
anemometer 46
Antonov An-225 Mriya 65
Anzani, Alessandro 15;
  engine 15, 22, 28, 29
Arlandes, Marquis d' 8, 65
Armstrong Siddeley 49
Armstrong-Whitworth 39
Atlantic crossing 9, 32, 42, 67
autogiro 48–49, 70
automatic pilot 32, 40, 70
Avro Vulcan bomber 39
BAe 146 34–35
ballast, airship 57;
  balloon, 8, 55
  glider 59
ballonet, airship 56–57, 70
balloon, basket 8–9, 54–55, 64, 65
  burner, 55
  envelope 54
  festivals 68
  gas 8–9, 54
  hot-air 8, 54–55
  inflation 9, 54;
  load ring 9, 55
bank-link indicator 47
banking 14, 27, 41, 42, 47
barometer, 9
Bell, Alexander 11
Bell JetRanger 50–51, 52–53
Bell X-1 rocket plane 36
Bennett, Bill 62
Besnier 6
biplane 18–21, 24, 43, 65, 70
black box see flight data recorder
blast-valve, balloon 55

Blériot, Louis 14–15, 18, 28, 29, 40, 66
  Type XI 14–15, 22
  body bag 60
Boeing 247D 32–33
  707 35
  747 35, 45, 64, 65
  787 35
Boeing, William Edward 67
bomber plane 20, 24, 42
boom, helicopter 52–53
bracing 21, 23, 24, 32;
brakes 38
Breitling Orbiter 3 64
Bristol Fighter 18–21
Brown, Arthur 32, 42, 67
Bumble Bee Two 65

CDE

Camm, Sidney 24, 66
Cayley, George 10, 52, 66
Cessna 172E Skyhawk 27
Chanute, Octave 11
Charles, Jacques 8
Chauvière 15
Cierva C-30 48–49
  Juan de la, 48–49, 66
Clément-Bayard II 9
climbing 42, 47, 50, 63,
  airship 57
  balloon 9, 55
  helicopter 50
clothing for flying 16–17
cockpit 14, 42–43, 45, 59, 62, 70 see also glass cockpit
Comper Swift 27
Concorde, the 36, 37, 65
control 14, 40–41
  column, 19, 40–41, 42–43, 71
  electronic 34
  yoke 45, 59
Cornu, Paul 52, 64
Daedalus 6
Dandrieux 53
de Havilland Comet 35
  Dragon, 33
  Moth 62
  Tiger Moth 43
de Havilland, Geoffrey 67
de Laroche, Baroness Raymonde 64
de Rozier, Jean-Francois Pilâtre 65
Deperdussin 22, 38, 42
descent, airship 57
  balloon 9
  helicopter 50
dogfight 19, 23
dope 20, 24, 70
Douglas, Donald Wills 67
Douglas DC-8 35
drag 18, 21, 24, 25, 32, 34, 58, 59, 70
hinges, 49, 51
Earhart, Amelia 64, 67
Eipper Quicksilver 61

elevator 12, 13, 15, 20, 21, 27, 40, 57, 59, 70
Elliott altimeter 47
engine, petrol 12, 13, 26, 28
  piston 28, 29
  radial, 29, 33
  rotary, 29
  steam 12
  water-cooled 28, 29
  see also jet engine
English Channel, crossing 7, 14–15, 28, 66
ENV engine 28
Éole 13, 66

FG

Fairey-Reed 25, 31
fighter planes 19
fin 27, 59
flap 20, 34, 35, 45
flapping wings 6–7
Flettner, Anton 52
flight data recorder 47
flight deck 32, 44–45, 56
flight simulators 44–45, 69
floats 25, 38
Flyer 14, 27, 48, 64
flying boat 21, 33, 70
Focke, Heinrich 52
Fokker, Anthony 67
Fokker Triplane 18
Fossett, Steve 64
fuselage, 22, 23, 26, 27, 34, 59, 70
Giffard, Henri 9, 66
glass cockpit 44, 70
glide ratio 58, 60
glider 10–11, 58–59, 60, 70
Gloster E28/39, 36
Gnome engine 23
gondola, airship 56–57, 70
Gossamer Albatross 7
gyroscope 45, 46–47

HIJK

Handley Page Heracles 33
hang-glider 10, 60–61, 62, 70
  microlight, 62
Hawker Hart 24, 39
Heinkel, Ernst Heinrich 67
Hele-Shaw-Beacham propeller 31
helicopter 48, 50–51, 52–53, 64, 70
helmet, flying 17
Henson, William 12–13
Hindenburg 56
Hispano-Suiza engine 19
horizon, artificial 45, 46–47, 70
hovering 50
Hughes H-4 Hercules 65
Icarus 6
Immelmann, Max 18, 67

Imperial Airways, 33
inclinometer 42
Instone Shipping Line 32
instruments 42–43, 44–45, 46–47, 62
  digital 26
Integrale propeller 31
jet aircraft 36, 38, 39
  jetliner 38, 39, 44–45, 67
  jet engine 28, 31, 34–35, 36–37, 51
  propfan 31
  turbofan 34–35, 36–37, 65, 71
  turbojet 36, 65, 71;
  turboprop 29, 36, 71
  turboshaft 51
Johnson, Amy 67
joystick see control column
jumbo jet see Boeing 747
Junkers, Hugo 67
Kanellopoulos, Kanellos 64
Kingsford Smith, Charles 32, 67
kite 10, 11, 60

LMNO

Landelle, Gabriel de la 52
landing 34, 39, 43
  airship 57
  approach 45, 47
  cushion 8
  gear 38–39
  lights 44
  skid 38, 51
  wheels 38–39
Lang propeller 31
Langley Samuel Pierpoint 13
Leonardo da Vinci 6–7
lift 11, 40, 71
Lilienthal, Otto 10–11, 60, 66
Lindbergh, Charles 26, 32, 64, 67
Lockheed, Allan Haines 67
longerons 20, 71
Macchi 25
Mach see sound, speed of
machine-gun 19, 20
  timing 19, 23, 31
magneto 32
microlight 26, 62–63, 71
monocoque 23, 24, 71
monoplane 15, 18, 22, 24, 25, 32, 33, 39, 62, 64, 71
Montgolfier brothers 8, 54, 64, 65, 66
Mortara, Riccardo 64
navigation 16, 34, 44–45, 46–47
ornithopter 6–7, 71

PQR

Pacific crossing 32, 67
parachute 10, 60

Paragon propeller 30
Passat, Maurice 7
passenger aircraft 32 comfort 33, 34–35
Paulhan, Louis 16
Pénaud, Alphonse 53
Pegoud, Adolphe 16
Phillips, Horatio 30
Pitcairn autogyro 48
pitch 40–41, 63
  collective pitch 50
  cyclic pitch 50
  helicopter controls 50–51, 52, 53
pitot tube 46
Pobjoy engine 27
Porsche engine 57
Post, Wiley 67
Pratt and Whitney
  Wasp engine 33
pressurized cabin 33, 34–35
Prevost, Maurice 64
propeller, 12, 18, 24, 25, 26, 29, 30, 49, 57, 62, 65, 71
  variable pitch, 31, 33
propfan engine see jet engine
Reed, S. A. 31
Roberts, Mario-Noel 8
Rockwell Sabreliner 64, 65
Rogallo, Francis 60
roll 14, 40–41, 71
Rolls-Royce R 25
  Kestrel 24
  Tay 36–37
  rotary flight 48–49, 50–51, 52–53
Rotax engine 26, 62
Rotherham pump 18
rotor blade 49, 50–51, 52–53
  pitch 50–51, 52
rudder, 13, 15, 19, 20, 21, 27, 40–41, 50, 53, 57, 59 bar 40–41, 42, 43

ST

Sablier, Georges 53
sailplane see glider
Santos-Dumont, Alberto 62
Saunders-Roe Princess 29
Scarff swivel ring 20, 71
Schleicher K23 58–59
Schneider Trophy 25, 64
Seguin brothers 29
Short Sarafand 21
Sidcot suit 16
sighting string, 47
Sikorsky, Igor 52–53, 66
  R-4 52–53
  VS-300, 52, 66
  XR-4 53
skin 32, 34, 35
Skyship 500 HL 56–57
Snowbird 26–27
Solar Wings Pegasus Q 62
Sopwith Pup 23

sound, speed of 36, 37, 46, 71
speed-bar, hang-glider 61
ultralight 63
Sperry, Elmer Ambrose 46, 66
spin 40
Spirit of St. Louis 26, 64
Spitfire see Supermarine
spoiler 27, 34
stall 27, 39, 40, 43
statoscope 9
Steam Airliner 52
stringers, fuselage 35
Stringfellow 12–13
strut 20–21, 23, 71
Sunbeam 31
supercharger, engine 25
Supermarine S6/S6B, 25
  Spitfire 39
swashplate 50–51, 52
tail-rotor 50, 52–53
tailplane 12, 21, 27, 33, 40, 59, 71
Tatlin, Vladimir 7
thermal 58
throttle, engine 42, 43, 44
tires 39
torque reaction 50, 53
trike, microlight 62
triplane 18, 71

UVWYZ

ultralight 26, 62–63, 71
undercarriage 14, 19, 22, 24, 26, 32, 38–39, 71
  retracting 32–33, 38–39
unducted fan engine 31
Vickers Vimy 42
Virgin Atlantic GlobalFlyer 64
von Ohain, Hans 36, 66
warp, wing 14, 22, 23
WAE 342 Hurricane engine 29
Whittle, Frank 36, 66
winch-launch 58
windscreen 42, 43
wing 6–7, 10–11, 12, 14–15, 18, 20–21, 24, 26–27, 32–33, 34, 40, 43, 48–49, 59
  camber 11, 13, 23, 12, 20
  covering 7, 11, 12, 14, 20–21
  spars 11, 63
World War I 17, 18–21, 31, 32, 42, 47, 56
World War II 32, 38, 39, 46, 48, 53, 59
Wotan propeller 31
Wright, Orville and Wilbur 11, 14, 27, 30, 46, 48, 52, 66
yaw 40–41, 71
Yeager, Chuck 36, 67
Yost, Ed, 54
Zeppelin, 9, 56, 57 66
  New Technology 57

Acknowledgments

The publisher would like to thank:
Aeromega Helicopters, Stapleford, England: pp.50–51, 52–53; Airship Industries, London: pp. 56–57, and especially Paul Davie and Sam Eller; Bristol Old Vic Theatre, Bristol, England, for studio space: pp. 54–55, 60–61, 62–63, and especially Stephen Rebbeck; British Aerospace, Hatfield: pp. 34–35, 44–45; Cameron Balloons, Bristol, England: pp. 54–55, and especially Alan Noble; Musée des Ballons, Forbes' Chateau de Balleroy, Calvados, France: pp. 8–9; Noble Hardman Aviation, Crickhowell, Wales: pp. 26–27; Penny and Giles, Christchurch, England: p. 47 (flight data recorder); RAF Museum, Hendon, London: pp. 16–17, 23, 24, 29, 38–39, 48–49, 52–53, and especially Mike Tagg; SkySport Engineering, Sandy, Bedford, England: pp. 18–19, 20–21; Tim Moore and all the team at SkySport; Rolls-Royce, Derby, England: pp. 36–37; Solar Wings Limited, Marlborough, England: pp. 60–61, 62–63, and especially John Fack; The Hayward Gallery, London, and Tetra Associates: pp. 6–7; The London Gliding Club, Dunstable, England: pp. 59–59, and especially Jack Butler;

The Science Museum, London: pp. 10–11, 12–13, 25, 28–29, 30–31, 39, 40, 46–47, and especially Peter Fitzgerald; The Science Museum, Wroughton, England: pp. 32–33, and especially Arthur Horsman and Ross Sharp; The Shuttleworth Collection, Old Warden Aerodrome, Bedford, England: pp. 14–15, 22, 38, 40–41, 42–43, and especially Mike Tagg; John Bagley of the Science Museum for his help with the text; Lester Cheeseman for his desktop publishing expertise; Ian Graham for his assistance on the paperback edition.
Illustration Mick Loates, Peter Bull
Proofreading Miranda Smith
Wallchart Peter Radcliffe, Steve Setford
Clipart CD Jo Little, Lisa Stock, Jessamy Wood

Picture credits
The publisher would like to thank the following for their kind permission to reproduce their photographs:

(Key: a–above; b–below/bottom; c–center; f–far; l–left; r–right; t–top)

Airbus UK: AIRBUS S.A.S. 2009 - All rights reserved Concept by EIAI 68cr; **Airship Industries:** 57br; **Alamy Images:** Peter Titmuss 65br; **Austin J. Brown:** 27tr, 35tr, 36tr, 55cl; **aviation-images.com:** Mark Wagner 35fcla, 68bl; **British Aerospace:** 35br, cr; **Bennie Bos/www.hotair.nl** 68tl; **Damien Burke/HandmadeByMachine.com/photographersdirect. com:** 69clb; **Corbis:** Stefano Rellandini/Reuters 53br, Galen Rowell 70tr, Karl Weatherly 70tl, Washington University 64br; **Getty Images:** Jonathan Daniel 65cl, Mark Wagner 68–69, Hulton Archive 67cra; **Michael Holford:** 10tc; **Hulton Picture Library:** 9tc, 9br, 48tl, 52tr; **Mary Evans Picture Library:** 6tc, 6bl, 8bl, 11tr, 11br, 14lc; 15rc, 20tl, 21br, 26tl, 32tl, 33br, 39br, 481c, 52tl, 53tl, 56tl, 64tr, G. B. Edwards 66cl; courtesy Northrop Grumman Corp: 65bl; **Popperfoto** 39tr; 53tr; 64bl, 67tl, 67clb; **Quadrant:** 49bc; **Retrograph Archive:** 61c; **Reuters:** 67br; **Rex Features:** 70–71; Dennis Stone 71tr, Mega 70bl; **Robert Hunt Library:** 18bl; **Science Museum/Science & Society Picture Library:** 10bl, 12bc, 13br, 69cla; **Fred Sgrosso:** 68tr; **Solar Wings:** 60bl, 62bl; **TopFoto:** 64tl, 66cra, 66bl;

Jerry Young: 55bl; **Zefa:** 37br, 60tr, br; **courtesy ZLT, www.zeppelinflug.de:** 57tr

Wallchart:
The Aviation Picture Library: Austin J. Brown clb (Bell X-1); **Corbis:** Swim Ink 2, LLC ftr; **Dorling Kindersley:** Courtesy of The Shuttleworth Collection, Bedfordshire cla (LVG CVI); Imperial War Museum, London fcl; **Getty Images:** Frank Cezus cb (Boeing 747); Mark Harwood bc; Library of Congress / Science Faction tl ('Flyer'); Taxi bl (balloon).

Jacket:
Front **Corbis:** Reuters / Jack Dabaghian ca; Jim Sugar (main image). **Dorling Kindersley:** Avionics Mobile Services Ltd, Watford tr.

All other images © Dorling Kindersley.
For further information see:
www.dkimages.com